MW00513040

SAS® Introductory Guide for Personal Computers, Release 6.03 Edition

SAS Institute Inc.
SAS Campus Drive
Cary, NC 27513

The correct bibliographic citation for this manual is as follows: SAS Institute Inc. *SAS® Introductory Guide for Personal Computers, Release 6.03 Edition.* Cary, NC: SAS Institute Inc., 1988. 111 pp.

SAS® Introductory Guide for Personal Computers, Release 6.03 Edition

1st printing, May 1988
2nd printing, June 1990
3rd printing, July 1991

Note that text corrections may have been made at each printing.

The SAS® System is an integrated system of software providing complete control over data access, management, analysis, and presentation. Base SAS software is the foundation of the SAS System. Products within the SAS System include SAS/ACCESS® SAS/AF® SAS/ASSIST® SAS/CALC™ SAS/CPE® SAS/DMI® SAS/EIS™ SAS/ETS® SAS/FSP® SAS/GRAPH® SAS/IML® SAS/IMS-DL/I® SAS/OR® SAS/QC® SAS/REPLAY-CICS® SAS/SHARE® SAS/STAT® SAS/CONNECT™ SAS/DB2™ SAS/INSIGHT™ SAS/PH-Clinical™ SAS/SQL-DS™ and SAS/TOOLKIT™ software. Other SAS Institute products are SYSTEM 2000® Data Management Software, with basic SYSTEM 2000, CREATE™ Multi-User™ QueX™ Screen Writer™ and CICS interface software; NeoVisuals® software; JMP® JMP Ahead™ JMP IN® and JMP SERVE® software; SAS/RTERM® software; the SAS/C® Compiler, and the SAS/CX® Compiler. MultiVendor Architecture™ and MVA™ are trademarks of SAS Institute Inc. *SAS Communications® SAS Training® SAS Views®* and the SASware Ballot® are published by SAS Institute Inc. All trademarks above are registered trademarks or trademarks, as indicated by their mark, of SAS Institute Inc.

A footnote must accompany the first use of each Institute registered trademark or trademark and must state that the referenced trademark is used to identify products or services of SAS Institute Inc.

The Institute is a private company devoted to the support and further development of its software and related services.

Doc SS1, Ver030.4, 050890

Contents

Illustrations

Screens

Tables

x

Credits

Documentation

Composition	Gail C. Freeman, Kelly W. Godfrey
Graphics	Michael J. Pezzoni
Proofreading	Bruce C. Brown, Reid J. Hardin, Michael H. Smith
Technical Assistance	Tom Disque, Craig Sampson, Curt Yeo
Technical Review	Deborah S. Blank, Brenda C. Kalt, Marian Saffer, Holly S. Whittle
Writing and Editing	Kathryn A. Council, Betty Fried, Carol A. Linden, Gary R. Meek, Rebeccah K. Neff, Judith K. Whatley

Software

The implementation of the PC version of the SAS System was led by John P. Sall (Senior Vice President), Robert L. Cross (Director of Core Development), with the guidance of James H. Goodnight (President). Detailed credits for the display manager, supervisor, DATA step, and other system components are in the front of the *SAS Language Guide for Personal Computers, Release 6.03 Edition*. Detailed credits for the procedures in the SAS System are in the front of the *SAS Procedures Guide, Release 6.03 Edition*. The PC version of the SAS System was developed on an Apollo domain network, as well as on IBM PCs.

Acknowledgment

Special thanks to Jane T. Helwig, now at Seasoned Systems, Inc., Chapel Hill, NC, who wrote the original *SAS Introductory Guide*.

Using This Book

Purpose of This Book

The goal of the *SAS Introductory Guide for Personal Computers, Release 6.03 Edition* is to help you learn enough to use the SAS System on personal computers to get the answers you need quickly. It is one of three manuals that document Release 6.03 of base SAS software for personal computers. The other books in the set are the *SAS Language Guide for Personal Computers, Release 6.03 Edition* and the *SAS Procedures Guide, Release 6.03 Edition.*

This book assumes that you know how to turn on your PC and some of the basic functions of the various keys. For example, you should know how to move the cursor and where the function keys are located. Many keys on your keyboard have special meanings when you are using the SAS System. (Some of these will be explained later.)

How This Book Is Organized

The book is divided into three parts.

Part I, **Introduction to the SAS System on a PC**, includes two chapters.

- Chapter 1 introduces you to the SAS System and to the data and task used in the sample SAS session in Chapter 2.
- As you read Chapter 2, follow along at your PC to become familiar with the SAS Display Manager System.

Part II, **SAS Language**, describes the SAS statements you will need to get your data into a SAS data set and to analyze the data.

- In Chapter 3 you learn several ways to get your data into a SAS data set.
- Chapter 4 describes ways to manipulate and rearrange your data.
- In Chapter 5 you learn how to use SAS procedures to analyze your data.
- Chapter 6 describes the SAS procedures SORT, PRINT, FREQ, and MEANS.

The last two chapters make up Part III, **Environment for Your SAS Session.**

- Chapter 7 gives enough details about the SAS Display Manager System so that you can begin using the SAS System on your PC.
- Chapter 8 describes the SAS Procedure Menu System, a convenient way to use SAS procedures without having to remember the details of the control language.

How to Use This Book

Before you try to run the examples in this book, you should check with the SAS Software Representative at your site to make sure that Release 6.03 of base SAS software has been installed on your personal computer and that the DOS PATH command points to the \SAS directory.

If you are a new SAS user, you should read Chapters 1 and 2 and all of Part II, which will help you understand some of the fundamentals of the SAS language.

Chapter 3 ends with sections on special topics—subjects that not every user needs. These sections are enclosed in a blue box for easy reference. You may want to skip these sections until you need these topics for your application.

To learn how to use the SAS Display Manager System and the Procedure Menu System, you should read Part III.

After you are familiar with SAS terminology and concepts, you can quickly advance to the *SAS Language Guide* and the *SAS Procedures Guide*.

If you are already familiar with the SAS language, you should read Chapters 1 and 2; then you may want to skip ahead to Part III to learn more about using display manager and the Procedure Menu System.

Typographical Conventions

The following type styles are used in this book:

roman type	is the basic type style used for most text.
italic type	is used to define new terms and to indicate items in statement syntax that you need to supply.
bold type	is used to indicate that you must use the exact spelling and form shown in models of statements or commands. Bold type is also used refer you to other sections (either in the same or in other chapters). In addition, sentences of extreme importance are in bold type.
code	is used to show examples of SAS statements.

SAS code   Examples of SAS code are shown in lowercase type. You can enter your own SAS code in lowercase, uppercase, or a mixture of the two. The SAS System always changes your variable names to uppercase, but character variable values remain in lowercase on printed or displayed output if you have entered them that way. Enter any titles and footnotes exactly as you want them to appear on your output.

Using the ENTER and Control Keys

In some chapters you are asked to type a command and press ENTER. On your keyboard this key may be labeled with the word Enter or with a bent arrow. In addition, you may be asked to press the CTRL key; this key may be labeled Ctrl on your keyboard. For more information on using SAS software with your keyboard, see Chapter 10, "SAS Display Manager System," in the *SAS Language Guide for Personal Computers, Release 6.03 Edition*.

INTRODUCTION TO THE SAS® SYSTEM ON A PC

Starting with the SAS® System

Sample SAS® Session

Chapter 1

Starting with the SAS® System

INTRODUCING THE SAS SYSTEM

What Is the SAS System?

The SAS System is a software system for data analysis and report writing. A software system is a group of computer programs that work together. With base SAS software you can store data values and retrieve them, modify data, compute simple statistics, and create reports all in one SAS session.

Other SAS software provides graphics, forecasting, data entry, and sophisticated statistics. All are available in one system.

INTRODUCING THE TASK

The SAS System works with data. The data must be in a SAS data set to use SAS procedures to analyze them. Before you run a SAS session to perform a task, you need to understand how your data relate to a SAS data set. Then you can relate your task to the parts of a SAS session.

Let's say that you work for a company that manufactures two kinds of business machines—small business machines like typewriters and copiers, and computers. For each product line you have a sales staff supporting all four regions of the country.

You maintain a file of information about each sales representative including last name, sales region, machine type, and year-to-date sales.

A summary of your data is shown in **Table 1.1**.

Table 1.1   SAS Data Set Listing of Data Values

Name	Year-to-date sales	Region	Machine type
Stafer	9664	east	SM
Young	22969	east	SM
Stride	27253	east	SM
Topin	86432	east	C
Spark	99210	east	C
Vetter	38928	west	C
Curci	21531	west	SM
Marco	79345	west	C
Greco	18523	west	SM
Ryan	32915	west	SM
Tomas	42109	west	SM
Thalman	94320	south	C
Moore	25718	south	SM
Allen	64700	south	C
Stelam	27634	south	SM
Farlow	32719	north	SM
Smith	38712	north	SM
Wilson	97214	north	C

Data values   Each item in **Table 1.1**—the name 'Stafer', the region 'south', the sales amount 97214—is a *data value*. The data value describing the machine type is 'SM' for small machines and 'C' for computers.

Observations   The information about each sales representative—name, sales, region, type of machine sold—makes up an *observation*. Each row in **Table 1.1** corresponds to an observation.

Variables   In **Table 1.1** each kind of information forms a column; the values in each column make up a *variable*. The names make up the name variable, the sales amounts are the sales variable, and so on. As you describe your data to the SAS System, you name each variable. Suppose you call the sales representatives' last names SALESREP; year-to-date sales, SALES; the regions, REGION; and the types of machines they sell, MACHINE. The name you choose can contain from one to eight characters. It can contain numbers and letters, but it must begin with a letter.

Data sets   Most collections of data are made up of many observations, each containing several variables. These collections are SAS *data sets*. All the sales information in **Table 1.1** makes up a data set. The data set has eighteen observations and four variables.

Getting data into a form the SAS System can read   There are several ways you could have had the SAS System read your data in the example above. You could have typed the information at your keyboard, stored it on disk, and then described it to the SAS System; or you could have entered it directly into a SAS data set. Perhaps the data in **Table 1.1** were already stored on another computer system.

All of these ways are described in the chapter "Getting Your Data into a SAS Data Set." In the sample session in the next chapter, you will learn one of the ways. Now you are ready to decide what you want the SAS System to do for you.

WHAT DO YOU WANT TO DO?

Before you can put together a SAS session, you need an idea of what you want the SAS System to do. Let's say that you want these results about your sales data:

- You want SAS to display your data after they have been organized into a SAS data set.
- You want to know the number of sales representatives in each region and how many sell each type of machine.
- You want average sales for each machine type.

Follow the discussion in the next chapter and see how you can get your results using the SAS System.

Sample SAS®
Session

To begin your SAS session, find the C> prompt on your screen, type the command

    sas

and press the ENTER key. This key also functions as the carriage-return key.

THE SAS DISPLAY MANAGER SYSTEM

The first thing you see is a set of windows that make up the SAS Display Manager System. The display manager is the interface between you and the SAS System. You use display manager to enter commands and SAS statements to submit to the SAS System and view your results.

When you first enter the system, your terminal screen looks like **Screen 2.1**.

The display manager divides your computer screen into windows corresponding to parts of your SAS session. You move among windows in the display manager system and execute SAS statements using display manager commands. You can type the command on the command line of any window and then press ENTER to submit the command. Or you can press a function key that has been defined to execute the command.

```
┌OUTPUT───────────────────────────────────────────────────────────────┐
│Command ===>                                                          │
│                                                                      │
│                                                                      │
│                                                                      │
│                                                                      │
│                                                                      │
│                                                                      │
├LOG──────────────────────────────────────────────────────────────────┤
│Command ===>                                                          │
│                                                                      │
│NOTE: Copyright(c) 1985,86,87 SAS Institute Inc., Cary, NC 27512-8000, U.S.A.│
│NOTE: SAS (r) Proprietary Software Release 6.03                       │
│      Licensed to SAS Institute Inc., Site 00000000.                  │
│                                                                      │
├─────────────────────────────────────────────────────────────────────┤
│Command ===>                                                          │
│                                                                      │
│00001                                                                 │
│00002                                                                 │
│00003                                                                 │
└─────────────────────────────────────────────────────────────────────┘
```

Screen 2.1   A SAS Display Manager System Screen

Starting at the bottom, the PROGRAM EDITOR is where you enter the SAS statements to be executed.

The LOG window displays messages from the SAS System as well as your SAS statements as they are executed. When you first enter the SAS System, the LOG window tells you the SAS release number and the name of the company authorized by SAS Institute to run this version on its microcomputers.

The OUTPUT window is where results output by SAS procedures are displayed.

There are other special-purpose windows that can be called using display manager global commands described in the chapter, "SAS Display Manager System." These windows are discussed in the *SAS Language Guide for Personal Computers, Release 6.03 Edition*.

To begin learning about the SAS Display Manager System and how you use it to run your interactive SAS sessions, let's start by learning how function keys are used. Then we will run a SAS session to create the SAS data set described in the last chapter.

FUNCTION KEYS

Function keys are the ten keys on your keyboard labeled F1 through F10. As their name implies, they can be "programmed" to perform functions for using the display manager system. Pressing a function key that has been defined as a command has the same effect as entering the command at the keyboard. By combining these ten keys with other keys (such as the shift and control keys), you can program up to 92 different functions.

The KEYS Window

Enter the KEYS command on any command line

```
Command ===> keys
```

and press ENTER.

The KEYS window is displayed on the right side of the screen (**Screen 2.2**), partially covering other windows. The cursor appears on the command line of that window.

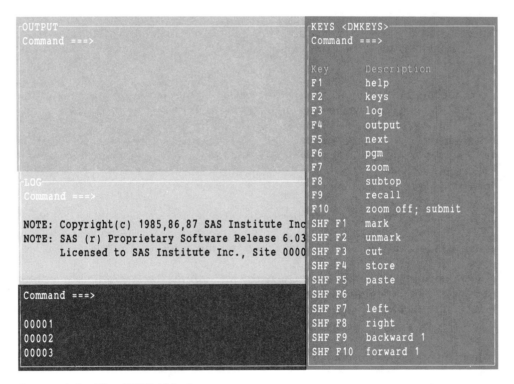

Screen 2.2   The KEYS Window

The KEYS window tells you how each function key is defined. The definitions shown in **Screen 2.2** are the default set of function key definitions. The first ten function key definitions, F1-F10, are some of the most commonly used commands. Some keys have not yet been given definitions; you can define those keys to be single commands or SAS statements, a combination of commands or statements, or even character strings that you plan to use.

Now you are ready to run a sample SAS session. To remove the KEYS window from the screen, enter END on the command line and press ENTER or press the SUBMIT function key, F10. (SUBMIT and END are equivalent commands.) You are returned to the original display manager screen.

RUNNING A SAS SESSION

You have information about your sales representatives. You want to display your data, look at counts of representatives by region and product, and find the average sales for each type of machine.

Entering SAS Statements

There are several ways to get your sales data into a form the SAS System can read. Since you have only a small amount of information, you can easily enter it at your keyboard.

To enter the SAS statements, move the cursor to the first numbered line in the PROGRAM EDITOR by pressing the carriage-return key.

Now enter your SAS statements. SAS statements are free form; they can be entered anywhere on the line with as many on a line as you want. A statement can continue over several lines. You can enter SAS statements in uppercase or lowercase letters. However, each statement **must** end with a semicolon.

In this example, one SAS statement is entered on each line of the PROGRAM EDITOR window (**Screen 2.3**). Each time you enter a SAS statement on the line, move to the beginning of the next line using the carriage-return key.

You can use the cursor keys on your keyboard to move the cursor back and forth among the SAS statements to make any necessary corrections or changes. This is possible since the statements are not submitted to the SAS System until you enter a command to submit them.

You can also use line commands to edit your SAS session more easily. Enter line commands over the numbers on the left side of the PROGRAM EDITOR window to do things like copy, move, delete, and repeat lines or blocks of lines. Some useful line commands are described in the "SAS Display Manager System" chapter.

To get additional lines on the screen, press the carriage-return key to scroll the window as in **Screen 2.4**.

```
OUTPUT
Command ===>
```

```
LOG
Command ===>

NOTE: Copyright(c) 1985,86,87 SAS Institute Inc., Cary, NC 27512-8000, U.S.A.
NOTE: SAS (r) Proprietary Software Release 6.03
      Licensed to SAS Institute Inc., Site 00000000.
```

```
PROGRAM EDITOR
Command ===>

00001 data sales;
00002     input salesrep $ sales region $ machine $;
00003     cards;
```

Screen 2.3   Using the PROGRAM EDITOR Window to Enter SAS Statements

```
OUTPUT
Command ===>
```

```
LOG
Command ===>

NOTE: Copyright(c) 1985,86,87 SAS Institute Inc., Cary, NC 27512-8000, U.S.A.
NOTE: SAS (r) Proprietary Software Release 6.03
      Licensed to SAS Institute Inc., Site 00000000.
```

```
PROGRAM EDITOR
Command ===>

00002     input salesrep $ sales region $ machine $;
00003     cards;
00004
```

Screen 2.4   Using the Carriage-Return Key to Get Additional Lines

Another way to get more lines is to "zoom" the PROGRAM EDITOR window using the ZOOM command so that the window fills the screen. Press F7 to fill the screen with the PROGRAM EDITOR window as in **Screen 2.5** so you can see more of your SAS program while you are editing it. (To "un-ZOOM" the window, or to reverse the effect of a ZOOM command, press the ZOOM key again. The screen returns to the previous arrangement.)

```
┌PROGRAM EDITOR─────────────────────────────────────────────────────────
│Command ===>
│
│00002     input salesrep $ sales region $ machine $;
│00003     cards;
│00004
│00005
│00006
│00007
│00008
│00009
│00010
│00011
│00012
│00013
│00014
│00015
│00016
│00017
│00018
│00019
│00020
│00021
│00022
│                                                              ─ZOOM─
```

Screen 2.5   Using the ZOOM Command to Fill the Screen

```
┌─PROGRAM EDITOR────────────────────────────────────────────────────────────────
│Command ===>
│
│00002     input salesrep $ sales region $ machine $;
│00003     cards;
│00004 Stafer     9664    east      SM
│00005 Young      22969   east      SM
│00006 Stride     27253   east      SM
│00007 Topin      86432   east      C
│00008 Spark      99210   east      C
│00009 Vetter     38928   west      C
│00010 Curci      21531   west      SM
│00011 Marco      79345   west      C
│00012 Greco      18523   west      SM
│00013 Ryan       32915   west      SM
│00014 Tomas      42109   west      SM
│00015 Thalman    94320   south     C
│00016 Moore      25718   south     SM
│00017 Allen      64700   south     C
│00018 Stelam     27634   south     SM
│00019 Farlow     32719   north     SM
│00020 Smith      38712   north     SM
│00021 Wilson     97214   north     C
│00022 run;
│                                                          ZOOM
└────────────────────────────────────────────────────────────────────────────────
```

Screen 2.6 SAS Statements and Data Lines in the PROGRAM EDITOR
Window

Now you can finish entering the SAS statements and data lines (**Screen 2.6**). Move
the cursor to each new line with the carriage-return key.

If you want to scroll to the top of the PROGRAM EDITOR window, press the PgUp
key on the numeric keypad on the right of the keyboard.

Now, let's take a look at each SAS statement briefly. More details about these
SAS statements and others are given in other chapters in this book.

DATA SALES;

The DATA statement tells SAS to begin creating a SAS data set named SALES. All
data must be in a SAS data set before you can use the SAS System to analyze
them. To create a SAS data set, you use a DATA step, a series of SAS statements
that begin with a DATA statement and describe the data to be included in the
data set.

INPUT SALESREP $ SALES REGION $ MACHINE $;

The INPUT statement tells SAS how the data values are arranged on the data lines and what the variable names are. SALESREP comes first, then SALES, REGION, and MACHINE. The listing of variable names in the INPUT statement tells SAS that the data are arranged on the data lines in the order listed, with at least one space between values. The dollar sign after SALESREP, REGION, and MACHINE tells SAS that these values contain alphabetic characters.

CARDS;

The CARDS statement tells SAS that the data lines come next. (Its name comes from the early days of computing when the statements and data were typed on computer cards and given to a computer operator to submit.)

data lines

When you enter the data, one observation per line, you must leave at least one blank between values. The chapter, "Getting Your Data Into a SAS Data Set" explains this simple form of input in more detail.

RUN;

The RUN statement tells the SAS System to execute the previous SAS statements. It signals the end of a step in the SAS session.

Submitting Your SAS Statements

When your data are entered correctly, you are ready to submit these statements and data to the SAS System and build your SAS data set. Watch what happens when you press SUBMIT, function key F10.

The PROGRAM EDITOR window returns to its previous size and is cleared of all statements. An "R" in the lower right corner of the window tells you that the step is running.

After the program has run, look at the LOG window to see the system messages about your session.

The SAS log tells you that your data set has eighteen observations and four variables. The eighteen observations correspond to each sales representative; the four variables are those read by the INPUT statement. The log also tells you the amount of time the SAS System used to process the step. Press the LOG function key to move the cursor to the LOG window, and use the PgUp and PgDn keys to view all of the log if necessary. Or zoom the LOG window.

Not a Perfect Session

If the LOG window shows that you made some errors when you entered your SAS statements, you must rerun the DATA step before you can continue. Press F6 to return to the PROGRAM EDITOR window; display the previous statements submitted with the RECALL key, F9; and correct any errors. Then press F10 to resubmit the statements.

```
┌OUTPUT─────────────────────────────────────────────────────────
Command ===>




┌LOG────────────────────────────────────────────────────────────
Command ===>

    3    cards;
   22    run;
NOTE: The data set WORK.SALES has 18 observations and 4 variables.
NOTE: The DATA statement used 16.00 seconds.
┌PROGRAM EDITOR──────────────────────────────────────────────────
Command ===>

00001
00002
00003
```

Screen 2.7 LOG Screen Showing Messages

Analyzing the Data

Now you are ready to do some analysis on the data. SAS procedures (nicknamed PROCs) are used to process data in SAS data sets. There are procedures for all kinds of analysis from listings of your data to simple statistics to printing reports.

You first want to display the values in your data set SALES in an organized form with column headings, something for the PRINT procedure to do. Then you want to get a count of sales representatives in each region selling each machine type, an exercise for the FREQ procedure.

Next you want to look at average sales for each product line. To do that you need to rearrange your data set so that sales representatives selling each product line are grouped together. So you use PROC SORT to rearrange your data, then PROC MEANS to look at average sales.

Return to the PROGRAM EDITOR window by pressing the PGM function key, F6. Note that the previous SAS statements used to build the data set SALES no longer appear on the screen.

Enter SAS statements to analyze your data set on the blank screen (**Screen 2.8**). The carriage-return key moves the cursor to each new line.

```
┌PROGRAM EDITOR──────────────────────────────────────────────────
│Command ===>
│
│00001 proc print;
│00002 run;
│00003 proc freq;
│00004    tables region*machine;
│00005 run;
│00006 proc sort;
│00007    by machine;
│00008 run;
│00009 proc means;
│00010    by machine;
│00011 run;
│00012
│00013
│00014
│00015
│00016
│00017
│00018
│00019
│00020
│00021
│                                                    ZOOM
```

Screen 2.8   SAS Statements to Analyze Data Set

Let's examine these SAS statements.

PROC PRINT;

The PROC PRINT statement asks SAS to display the data values in the data set just created. The word PROC signals the beginning of a PROC step, a series of statements that describe the analysis to be performed. The word PRINT names the SAS procedure you want to use. This PROC step consists of just the PROC PRINT statement and a RUN statement.

There are four PROC steps in this series of statements. Each one requests a SAS procedure to perform a specific task.

RUN;

The RUN statement tells SAS to run the preceding step. There is a RUN statement after every PROC step in this series of statements.

PROC FREQ;

The PROC FREQ statement asks SAS for frequency counts.

TABLES REGION*MACHINE;

The TABLES statement describes the table containing frequencies. TABLES REGION*MACHINE asks for a two-way table showing a count of sales representatives in each region by machine types.

PROC SORT;

The PROC SORT statement asks SAS to sort the data set.

BY MACHINE;

The BY statement describes how you want the data sorted. This statement tells SAS to rearrange the data so that sales representatives selling a particular type of machine are grouped together.

PROC MEANS;

The PROC MEANS statement requests simple statistics on numeric variables.

BY MACHINE;

The BY MACHINE statement tells the MEANS procedure to calculate the simple statistics in groups, in this case, grouping by machine type.

To send these statements to the SAS System, press the SUBMIT function key, F10. You see the R in the lower right corner appear and reappear as each PROC step is executed.

You can view the results produced by these procedures by moving to the OUTPUT window (use the OUTPUT function key, F4). Then enter the TOP command to scroll to the beginning of the procedure output and zoom the window (F7) to see as much of the output as possible (**Screen 2.9**).

The PROC PRINT statement produced what you see in **Screen 2.9**. Your sales data appear here in an organized form, with each column labeled. The column labeled OBS contains the number of each observation. Use the PgDn key to scroll to the next page of output (**Screen 2.10**).

In general, each procedure's output begins at the top of a new page rather than following the previous procedure's output on the same page. If you use a ZOOM command to enlarge the PROGRAM EDITOR window for entering SAS statements, submitting the statements to the SAS System cancels the command. After the SAS System executes those statements, the LOG, OUTPUT, and PROGRAM EDITOR windows are all visible.

```
OUTPUT
Command ===>

                              SAS                                    1

         OBS    SALESREP    SALES    REGION    MACHINE

          1     Stafer       9664    east        SM
          2     Young       22969    east        SM
          3     Stride      27253    east        SM
          4     Topin       86432    east        C
          5     Spark       99210    east        C
          6     Vetter      38928    west        C
          7     Curci       21531    west        SM
          8     Marco       79345    west        C
          9     Greco       18523    west        SM
         10     Ryan        32915    west        SM
         11     Tomas       42109    west        SM
         12     Thalman     94320    south       C
         13     Moore       25718    south       SM
         14     Allen       64700    south       C
         15     Stelam      27634    south       SM
         16     Farlow      32719    north       SM
         17     Smith       38712    north       SM
                                                      ZOOM
```

Screen 2.9   OUTPUT Window Showing First Page of Sales Data

```
OUTPUT
Command ===>

                              SAS                                    3

                    TABLE OF REGION BY MACHINE

         REGION        MACHINE

         Frequency|
         Percent  |
         Row Pct  |
         Col Pct  |C       |SM      |  Total
         ---------+--------+--------+
         east     |     2  |     3  |      5
                  | 11.11  | 16.67  |  27.78
                  | 40.00  | 60.00  |
                  | 28.57  | 27.27  |
         ---------+--------+--------+
         Total          7       11       18
                    38.89    61.11   100.00
         (Continued)
                                                      ZOOM
```

Screen 2.10   OUTPUT Window Showing PROC FREQ Output

Press the PgDn key to scroll through the pages of output. The MEANS procedure output follows the frequency table from PROC FREQ (**Screen 2.11** and **Screen 2.12**). The SORT procedure produces no printed output.

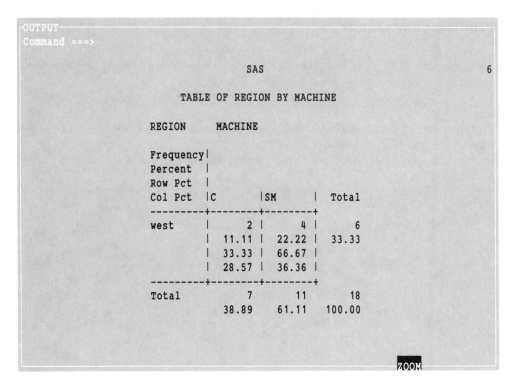

```
┌OUTPUT─────────────────────────────────────────────────────────
Command ===>

                              SAS                              6

              TABLE OF REGION BY MACHINE

          REGION      MACHINE

          Frequency|
          Percent  |
          Row Pct  |
          Col Pct  |C       |SM      | Total
          ---------+--------+--------+
          west     |    2 |    4 |      6
                   | 11.11 | 22.22 |  33.33
                   | 33.33 | 66.67 |
                   | 28.57 | 36.36 |
          ---------+--------+--------+
          Total         7       11        18
                      38.89    61.11    100.00

                                                    ▣ZOOM
```

Screen 2.11   Continuation of PROC FREQ Output

```
┌OUTPUT─────────────────────────────────────────────────────────
Command ===>

                              SAS                              7

          Analysis Variable : SALES


    --------------------------- MACHINE=C ----------------------------


    N Obs   N      Minimum        Maximum          Mean        Std Dev
    -----------------------------------------------------------------
       7    7    38928.00       99210.00       80021.29       21730.18
    -----------------------------------------------------------------

    --------------------------- MACHINE=SM ---------------------------


    N Obs   N      Minimum        Maximum          Mean        Std Dev
    -----------------------------------------------------------------
      11   11     9664.00       42109.00       27249.73        9236.48
    -----------------------------------------------------------------

                                                    ▣ZOOM
```

Screen 2.12   PROC MEANS Output

Printing Your Output

You can use the FILE command to save the information displayed in the OUTPUT window or to print it on your attached printer. To send the entire contents of the OUTPUT window to the printer attached to your PC, type

```
file 'prn:'
```

on the command line, as shown in **Screen 2.13**, and press ENTER. For more information on the FILE command, see Chapter 10, "SAS Display Manager System," in the *SAS Language Guide for Personal Computers*.

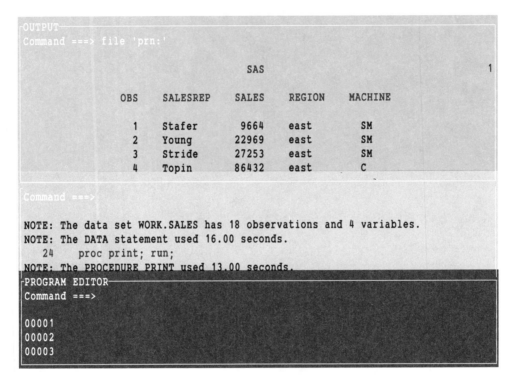

Screen 2.13   The FILE Command in the OUTPUT Window

Ending the SAS Session

When you are ready to end the SAS session, enter BYE on the command line of any window or enter the SAS statement

```
endsas;
```

on a line and press SUBMIT, F10. You are returned to the operating system.

Summary

In the sample SAS session in this chapter, you learned a way to get your data into a SAS data set so that you could analyze them. Then you looked at your data in several ways—using the procedures PRINT, FREQ, and MEANS. The environment for the session was the SAS Display Manager System.

But you ran the session without really understanding how the SAS System and display manager work. Part II of this manual, SAS LANGUAGE, describes the fundamentals of the SAS language, giving detailed explanations of some of the SAS statements you have just seen. For additional details about the environment for your session including display manager and the sample menu system, go to Part III, ENVIRONMENT FOR YOUR SAS SESSION.

SAS®
LANGUAGE

Getting Your Data into a SAS® Data Set

Shaping Your Data

Using SAS® Procedures

Rearranging, Displaying, and Summarizing
Your Data

24

Getting Your Data into a SAS® Data Set

Your data are in one of two forms: a form external to the SAS System or a SAS data set. If they are already in a SAS data set, then they are in a form the PC and the SAS System can read. If they are external to the SAS System, they may not be in a form the PC can read. (For example, they may be sales figures turned in on individual monthly sales reports, or they may be expense amounts that you have gathered from your own records.) In that case, you need to enter and store them in a file on your PC.

If your data are stored on your fixed disk or a diskette, then they are ready to read using your PC. If they are stored on disk or tape on the main computer, they must be downloaded to a file on your PC. Let's assume that your data are stored on your fixed disk or a diskette. (You may have entered the data onto a diskette using an editor. The last section in this chapter describes a way to do that using the PROGRAM EDITOR in the SAS System.)

Before we discuss the SAS statements used to create a SAS data set from data on your PC, let's briefly discuss SAS statements in general.

SAS STATEMENTS

The SAS System is run by a command language composed of SAS statements. SAS statements ask the SAS System to perform some activity.

The first word of a SAS statement is a keyword that tells SAS what activity you want to perform, for example, create a SAS data set, run a statistical procedure, or print a line of data. In the rest of the SAS statement, you give SAS more information about how you want the activity performed, for instance, what to name the new data set, which procedure to run, and how to arrange the line you want printed.

Every SAS statement ends with a semicolon. For example, consider this SAS statement:

```
data sales;
```

The first word, DATA, tells the SAS System to begin a step to create a SAS data set. The word SALES is the name you want to give the data set. The statement ends with a semicolon.

In the SAS statement

```
proc print;
```

the word PROC tells the SAS System to run a SAS procedure. PRINT is the name of the procedure that prints a SAS data set.

You can put more than one SAS statement on a line. For example, these statements:

```
data new;
   input x y z;
   cards;
```

could also be written as:

```
data new; input x y z; cards;
```

However, you may find it easier to understand your SAS programs when each statement occupies one line.

SAS statements can begin in any column on a line. For clarity, the examples in this book show the DATA, PROC, and RUN statements beginning in column 1; most other statements are indented.

DATA EXTERNAL TO THE SAS SYSTEM

Getting Your Data from a File to a SAS Data Set

To get your data from a DOS file into a SAS data set, you need these SAS statements:

- the DATA statement
- the INFILE statement
- the INPUT statement
- the RUN statement.

When you need to modify your data before you analyze them, you will also need the statements described in the next chapter.

The DATA Statement: Beginning a SAS Data Set

You use the DATA statement to tell the SAS System that you want to create a SAS data set. The DATA statement signals the beginning of a DATA step. A DATA step is a series of SAS statements that create a SAS data set.

The DATA statement begins with the word DATA and then gives the name you choose for the data set you are creating:

```
data sales;
```

You can choose any name you want for the data set name, as long as it has eight or fewer characters and begins with a letter. It is easier to understand the statements in your SAS program if you choose names that describe the contents of the data sets.

The DATA statement signals the beginning of a new step in your SAS program, so you want the DATA statement to appear after the RUN statement in a previous step or as the first statement in your session (**Screen 3.1**).

The INFILE Statement: Pointing to Your Data File

One of the things you have to tell the SAS System about your data is their location. You use the INFILE statement to point to your data file. The INFILE statement begins with the word INFILE and then gives a description of your file. The description following the keyword INFILE can be a filename in single quotes as in this example or it can be a fileref. (A fileref is a nickname for a file. The nickname is associated with a particular file in a FILENAME statement. See **The FILENAME Statement: Identifying Your Data File.**)

```
infile 'a:mydata.dat';
```

The INFILE statement says to the SAS System "Get the data from file MYDATA.DAT in drive A. Those are the data I will be describing in the DATA step."

The INFILE statement must appear after the DATA statement and before the INPUT statement describing each record or line of data.

```
┌PROGRAM EDITOR────────────────────────────────────────────────────────┐
│Command ===>                                                           │
│                                                                       │
│00001 data sales;                                                      │
│00002    infile 'a:mydata.dat';                                        │
│00003                                                                  │
│00004                                                                  │
│00005                                                                  │
│00006                                                                  │
│00007                                                                  │
│00008                                                                  │
│00009                                                                  │
│00010                                                                  │
│00011                                                                  │
│00012                                                                  │
│00013                                                                  │
│00014                                                                  │
│00015                                                                  │
│00016                                                                  │
│00017                                                                  │
│00018                                                                  │
│00019                                                                  │
│00020                                                                  │
│00021                                                                  │
│                                                            ─ZOOM───── │
└───────────────────────────────────────────────────────────────────── ┘
```

Screen 3.1   Getting Your Data into a SAS Data Set

The INPUT Statement: Describing Your Input Records to the SAS System

In the INPUT statement, you describe each record in your data file to the SAS System. The INPUT statement is important because SAS reads each data line or record using the description you give.

Suppose the sales information has been entered onto your diskette with the sales representative's last name in columns 1-8 of each line, year-to-date sales in columns 10-15, region in columns 19-23, and machine type in columns 29-30, as shown here:

```
COLS+----1----+----2----+----3----+----4----+----5----+---
Stafer    9664   east     SM
Young    22969   east     SM
Stride   27253   east     SM
Topin    86432   east     C
Spark    99210   east     C
Vetter   38928   west     C
  .
  .
  .
Wilson   97214   north    C
```

The INPUT statement follows the INFILE statement. The INFILE statement points to the file; the INPUT statement describes records in the file (**Screen 3.2**).

```
┌PROGRAM EDITOR──────────────────────────────────────────────────────┐
│Command ===>                                                         │
│                                                                     │
│00001 data sales;                                                    │
│00002     infile 'a:mydata.dat';                                     │
│00003     input salesrep $ 1-8 sales 10-15 region $ 19-23            │
│00004           machine $ 29-30;                                     │
│00005                                                                │
│00006                                                                │
│00007                                                                │
│00008                                                                │
│00009                                                                │
│00010                                                                │
│00011                                                                │
│00012                                                                │
│00013                                                                │
│00014                                                                │
│00015                                                                │
│00016                                                                │
│00017                                                                │
│00018                                                                │
│00019                                                                │
│00020                                                                │
│00021                                                           ─ZOOM─│
└─────────────────────────────────────────────────────────────────────┘
```

Screen 3.2   Using the INFILE and INPUT Statements

How to write the INPUT statement   The steps below use the sales data above to show how to write an INPUT statement.

1. Begin with the word INPUT:

    input

2. Choose a name for the first variable on each record. (Remember the naming rules: names must begin with letters and can have no more than eight characters.) Write the name you choose:

    input salesrep

3. Is the variable character or numeric? If its values contain letters or other non-numeric characters, it is a character variable. If it is a character variable, put a dollar sign after the variable name.

    input salesrep $

4. What columns do the data values occupy in the record? Write the number of the column where values of the variable begin, then write a dash, then the column where the value ends:

    input salesrep $ 1-8

It is important to give the entire range of columns where the variable's values might be found, even if not all the values occupy all the columns. For example, in the REGION field, 'east' occupies only four columns, but 'north' occupies all five columns.

If the data values for a variable occupy only one column on the data lines, put just the column's number. For example, suppose data values for a MACHINE were Cs and Ss, instead of C and SM, located in column 30 of the record. Then, an INPUT statement to read these values might be:

```
input machine $ 30
```

Repeat steps 2 through 4 for each variable that you want SAS to read. After you finish describing the data, put a semicolon to end the INPUT statement:

```
input salesrep $ 1-8 sales 10-15 region $ 19-23
      machine $ 29-30;
```

The INPUT statement is now complete.

Note that your INPUT statement is so long that it continues to a second line. When you have to use two lines to write the INPUT statement, do not split a variable name between two lines. Notice that the second line of the INPUT statement is indented so it is easier to read.

Special situations in the INPUT statement   The next three sections describe these special situations:

- You want to skip some of the data values in the record.
- Some of the data values are missing.
- You want to learn an easier way to write the INPUT statement.

Skipping data values   If your records contain values that you do not want the SAS System to read, then do not describe these variables in the INPUT statement. SAS reads only information you describe in the INPUT statement.

For example, if you needed only the SALESREP variable and REGION, you could use this INPUT statement:

```
input salesrep $ 1-8 region $ 19-23;
```

What happens if some data values are missing?   Often one or more data values are missing. For example, suppose a new sales representative named Smith was added to the file and had not yet made any sales. You have the rest of the information for Smith (his region and machine type), but no sales values.

If the columns that contain sales values (columns 10-15) are blank on the Smith record or if those columns contain a period, the SAS System treats Smith's sales as a *missing value*. Each SAS procedure has provisions for handling missing values. When the SAS System prints or displays data, a period is used for numeric variables to indicate a missing value, and a blank is used for missing character variables.

An easier way to write an INPUT statement   In the chapter "Sample SAS Session," we used a form of the INPUT statement that listed just the variable names. You can use that form of INPUT statement when your data satisfy these conditions:

- Each value on the data line is separated from the next value by at least one blank.
- Character values are eight characters or less, with no embedded blanks.
- Any missing data values are represented by a period rather than just blanks.

When your data meet these conditions, you can

- list variables in the INPUT statement in the order in which they appear on the input lines
- follow character variable names with a dollar sign ($)
- end the INPUT statement with a semicolon:

```
input salesrep $ sales region $ machine $;
```

When you write your INPUT statement this way, you must list all the variables on the input lines. It is not possible to skip any variables.

The CARDS Statement: Entering Data with Your SAS Statements

When you enter lines of data along with your SAS program, the CARDS statement immediately precedes the data lines. Its form is simply:

```
cards;
```

The CARDS statement tells the SAS System that the data lines come next. So put your data lines immediately after the CARDS statement (**Screen 3.3**).

```
┌PROGRAM EDITOR─────────────────────────────────────────────────────┐
│Command ===>                                                        │
│                                                                    │
│00001 data sales;                                                   │
│00002    input salesrep $ 1-8 sales 10-15 region $ 19-23            │
│00003          machine $ 29-30;                                     │
│00004    cards;                                                     │
│00005 Stafer    9664    east      SM                                │
│00006 Young     22969   east      SM                                │
│00007 Stride    27253   east      SM                                │
│00008 Topin     86432   east      C                                 │
│00009 Spark     99210   east      C                                 │
│00010 Vetter    38928   west      C                                 │
│00011 Curci     21531   west      SM                                │
│00012 Marco     79345   west      C                                 │
│00013 Greco     18523   west      SM                                │
│00014 Ryan      32915   west      SM                                │
│00015 Tomas     42109   west      SM                                │
│00016 Thalman   94320   south     C                                 │
│00017 Moore     25718   south     SM                                │
│00018 Allen     64700   south     C                                 │
│00019 Stelam    27634   south     SM                                │
│00020 Farlow    32719   north     SM                                │
│00021 Smith     38712   north     SM                                │
│                                                        ─ZOOM─      │
└────────────────────────────────────────────────────────────────────┘
```

Screen 3.3   Using the CARDS Statement

Notice that a CARDS statement replaces the need for an INFILE statement since the CARDS statement points to the data. The CARDS statement tells the SAS System, "Next come data lines."

Running the DATA step   When you want to signal to the SAS System that you are ready to run your SAS statements, use a RUN statement. The form of the RUN statement is

```
run;
```

When SAS sees a RUN statement it executes the statements just submitted.

Special Topic

The FILENAME Statement: Identifying Your Data File

If your data come from a file other than a SAS data set, you can describe your data file to the SAS System using a FILENAME statement. The FILENAME statement is an alternative to specifying the filename in the INFILE statement. It is convenient when you want to describe your file once and then refer to the file several times during the session.

In the FILENAME statement you associate a fileref with a description of your external file. A fileref is nothing more than a nickname for your file. It can be any name you choose so long as it begins with a letter and has no more than eight characters.

The FILENAME statement begins with the word FILENAME and then gives the fileref followed by the name of a data file in single quotes. For example,

```
filename saledat 'a:\mydata.dat';
```

SALEDAT is the fileref for the file A:\MYDATA.DAT.

When you use the name SALEDAT in another SAS statement, for example, with the statement

```
infile saledat;
```

the SAS System knows what file you are referring to.

A:\MYDATA.DAT tells the SAS System that the file is located on the diskette in drive A, is in the root directory of that diskette, has name MYDATA, and extension DAT. Refer to your operating system documentation for a description of filenames.

Make sure that when this FILENAME statement executes, the diskette containing the file identified by \MYDATA.DAT is loaded in drive A.

The FILENAME statement (and there can be more than one of them if you plan to use several different files in the same session) can appear anywhere in a SAS session as long as it appears before any statements that reference the same fileref.

It is usually a good idea to group your FILENAME statements at the beginning of your SAS program before you create any data sets.

Special Topic

Alternate Sources of Data

On the main computer   Suppose the data you want to analyze are stored on disk or tape on the main computer. How can you access the data from your PC?

You can download data from the main computer with the SAS DOWNLOAD procedure. The DOWNLOAD procedure is part of base SAS software. General information on PROC DOWNLOAD is in the *SAS Guide to the Micro-to-Host Link, Version 6 Edition,* and additional information for Release 6.03 is in Chapter 18, "The DOWNLOAD Procedure," *SAS Procedures Guide, Release 6.03 Edition.*

Once the data are downloaded to your PC, you can use the statements described in this chapter to create your SAS data set.

DBF or DIF Files   If you have data stored in dBASE II or dBASE III files, you can convert the data into a SAS data set by using PROC DBF. Data stored in the Data Interchange Format (DIF), which is used for Lotus 1-2-3 files, can be converted to SAS data sets by using PROC DIF.

In this example, a dBASE II file named MAIL.DBF is converted to a SAS data set. Since no FILENAME statement is specified, the last level of the filename is assumed to be DBF and the file is assumed to be in your current directory.

```
proc dbf db2=mail out=save.mail;
run;
```

In the next example, a DIF filename MAIL.DIF is converted to a SAS data set. Since no FILENAME statement is specified, the last level of the filename is assumed to be DIF, and the file is assumed to be in your current directory.

```
proc dif dif=mail out=save.mail;
run;
```

To make the best use of your data, PROC DBF and PROC DIF also let you convert SAS data sets to dBASE II, dBASE III, or Lotus 1-2-3 files. The SAS Procedures DBF and DIF are described in the *SAS Procedures Guide for Personal Computers.*

DATA IN A SAS DATA SET

The data you want to analyze could already be in the form of a SAS data set. They could be stored permanently as a SAS data set on your fixed disk or on diskette. In that case, it is not necessary to use a DATA step unless you want to modify or subset the data. You can go directly to a PROC step to analyze the data.

Creating Permanent SAS Data Sets

In the previous examples, the data sets you created were temporary. That is, they were available to use with SAS procedures just as long as you remained in the SAS session. When you ended your session, the data sets were deleted.

However, if you store data permanently as a SAS data set, then in a later job or session, you can go directly to your analysis without recreating the SAS data set.

To create a permanent SAS data set you simply give the data set a two-part name rather than a single name. The program shown in **Screen 3.4** is an example.

```
┌PROGRAM EDITOR──────────────────────────────────────────────────┐
│Command ===>                                                     │
│                                                                 │
│00001 data mysave.sales;                                         │
│00002    infile 'a:mydata.dat';                                  │
│00003    input salesrep $ 1-8 sales 10-15 region $ 19-23         │
│00004          machine $ 29-30;                                  │
│00005 run;                                                       │
│00006 proc print;                                                │
│00007 run;                                                       │
│00008                                                            │
│00009                                                            │
│00010                                                            │
│00011                                                            │
│00012                                                            │
│00013                                                            │
│00014                                                            │
│00015                                                            │
│00016                                                            │
│00017                                                            │
│00018                                                            │
│00019                                                            │
│00020                                                            │
│00021                                                      ZOOM  │
└─────────────────────────────────────────────────────────────────┘
```

Screen 3.4   Creating a Permanent SAS Data Set

This DATA step creates a SAS data set named MYSAVE.SALES. Giving a two-level name to the data set tells the SAS System to store the data set permanently. The first part of the name, MYSAVE, is a *libref* and is always associated with a directory using a LIBNAME statement. Librefs, like filerefs, can be any name you choose up to eight characters.

LIBNAME Statement: Telling SAS Where to Store Your SAS Data Set

If you are creating a SAS data set that you want to store permanently on a directory other than your current directory, you associate a libref with the directory using a LIBNAME statement. You tell the SAS System to store the data sets on the directory by giving the libref as the first-level name.

For example, the statement

```
libname old '\mydir\';
```

associates libref OLD with the directory MYDIR. The subsequent DATA statement

```
data old.january;
```

tells the SAS System to create a data set OLD.JANUARY and store it in the directory MYDIR.

Special Topic

SAS Data Sets Stored on the Main Computer

Suppose your permanent SAS data sets are stored on disk or tape on the main computer. If your PC can "talk" to the main computer, you can use the micro-to-mainframe link available with base SAS software in the SAS System for Personal Computers to access the data and run your SAS program in one of two ways.

You can use your PC as a terminal and link to the main computer to run your SAS program, or you can download the data set to diskette using the DOWNLOAD procedure. The micro-to-mainframe link is described in the *SAS Guide to the Micro-to-Host Link, Version 6 Edition*.

Special Topic

SAS Data Sets Output from a SAS Procedure

Sometimes SAS procedures create a new SAS data set containing all or part of the results from the analysis. Normally, an OUTPUT statement or an option in the PROC statement tells the procedure that you want a new data set and what to name it.

For example, PROC CORR can process an input SAS data set and create a new data set containing Pearson correlations and other statistics. The OUTP= option in the PROC CORR statement tells the procedure what to name the new data set.

```
proc corr data=basedata outp=corrdata;
run;
```

Data set CORRDATA is the most recently created SAS data set once this PROC step is executed.

Another example is the SORT procedure, which always creates a new, sorted data set. These statements tell the procedure to write the data set that has been sorted by NAME in a data set named SORTED.

```
proc sort data=unsorted out=sorted;
    by name;
run;
```

The SAS procedure descriptions in the *SAS Procedures Guide, Release 6.03 Edition*, tell you when a procedure can create a new SAS data set and what the contents of the data set are.

Special Topic

Full-Screen Entering of Data into a SAS Data Set

WINDOW and DISPLAY statements   The WINDOW and DISPLAY statements allow you to create your own data-entry windows for entering data into a SAS data set or for displaying data at your PC.

The WINDOW statement is used to give the design specifications for creating a window. For example, the following DATA step creates and displays a window with fields for entering a daily phone log:

```
data phone;
    window daily color=green rows=14 columns=52
    #1 a15 'Daily Telephone Log'
    #3  a1 'PHONE' a15 'NAME' a45 'TIME'
    #5 phonenum $char12. a15 name $char25. a45 lencall time8.;
    display daily;
run;
```

The WINDOW statement names the window DAILY; the COLOR= option gives the background color; ROWS= tells the number of rows; COLUMNS= tells the window's width in columns. #1 @15 tells the SAS System, "At row 1, column 15, put the string 'Daily Telephone Log'." The third row of the statement has three column headings: PHONE, NAME, and TIME. Row 5 contains the names of three SAS variables, PHONENUM, NAME, and LENCALL, whose values you enter to produce the log of calls.

If you are familiar with the SAS language, you will recognize the similarities between the WINDOW statement and the PUT statement. The WINDOW statement is described in the *SAS Language Guide for Personal Computers, Release 6.03 Edition.*

When the DISPLAY statement is executed, the window DAILY is displayed. At this point all the variables have missing values, so the fields for PHONENUM and NAME are blank and LENCALL is marked with a period (which indicates a numeric missing value to the SAS System). You can now enter values for the telephone number, name of the person called, and the length of the call in hours and minutes. When you fill out the last field, press ENTER. The SAS System stores those values as an observation in PHONE (the data set being created) and blanks out the fields so you can enter new values for the next observation. To complete the SAS data set and remove the window, enter END on the command line and press ENTER, or press the END function key. The SAS data set PHONE contains three variables (PHONENUM, NAME, and LENCALL) and the number of observations you entered. **Screen 3.5** shows the window named DAILY.

(continued on next page)

Special Topic

(continued from previous page)

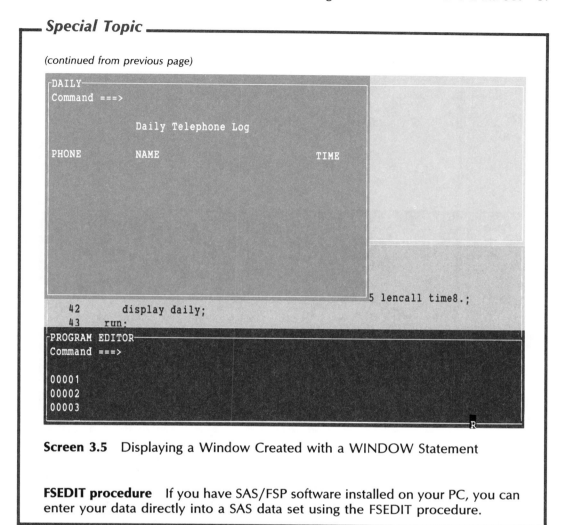

Screen 3.5   Displaying a Window Created with a WINDOW Statement

FSEDIT procedure   If you have SAS/FSP software installed on your PC, you can enter your data directly into a SAS data set using the FSEDIT procedure.

Special Topic

Using the SAS Editor to Store Data on a Local Disk

You can use the SAS editor to enter data and store them on your fixed disk or a diskette.

Just enter your data lines in the PROGRAM EDITOR window as shown in **Screen 3.6**.

```
┌PROGRAM EDITOR──────────────────────────────────────────────────────
│Command ===>
│
│00001 Stafer      9664    east      SM
│00002 Young      22969    east      SM
│00003 Stride     27253    east      SM
│00004 Topin      86432    east      C
│00005 Spark      99210    east      C
│00006 Vetter     38928    west      C
│00007 Curci      21531    west      SM
│00008 Marco      79345    west      C
│00009 Greco      18523    west      SM
│00010 Ryan       32915    west      SM
│00011 Tomas      42109    west      SM
│00012 Thalman    94320    south     C
│00013 Moore      25718    south     SM
│00014 Allen      64700    south     C
│00015 Stelam     27634    south     SM
│00016 Farlow     32719    north     SM
│00017 Smith      38712    north     SM
│00018 Wilson     97214    north     C
│00019
│00020
│00021
│                                           ─────ZOOM──
```

Screen 3.6   Entering Data Lines in the PROGRAM EDITOR Window

Move the cursor to the command line (use the HOME key) and enter

```
file 'a:sales.dat'
```

to store what is in the PROGRAM EDITOR window in a file named SALES.DAT on the diskette in drive A. The FILE command can give a fileref or the full name of the file where you want to store the data.

Note that the FILE command can also be used to save SAS programs for later use.

Shaping Your Data

If your data are ready to be analyzed and you do not need to subset the data or create new variables, then you can skip this chapter and go directly to the next two chapters on SAS procedures.

Often, however, data are not in the shape you want when you get them. For example, you may want to add new information to the data before you analyze them, or you may want to analyze only part of the original data. In that case, you can use additional statements in the DATA step to get your data in a form ready to analyze.

What Kinds of SAS Statements Are Available for Reshaping Data?

You use some SAS statements to work with the observations as they are read in, for example, to create new variables, delete observations, or select certain records.

Other SAS statements give the SAS System extra information about the data set you are creating, for example, the length you want the variable's values to have in the SAS data set or the format you want to use to print the variable's values.

And still other SAS statements change the order in which the SAS System executes program statements.

Such statements are *optional* in SAS programs. If present, they follow the DATA statement and precede the CARDS statement if there is one; otherwise they precede the RUN statement. Their order in the DATA step is sometimes important because of the way the SAS System creates a data set.

How the SAS System Creates a Data Set

To understand how to use these SAS statements, you first need to know how the SAS System creates a data set.

When the SAS System creates a data set, it goes through the following steps for each observation of your data:

1. The SAS System uses the description in the INPUT statement to read the observation.
2. It applies any other SAS statements in the DATA step to the data values in the observation.
3. It adds the observation to the data set being created.

It is important to understand that each statement in the DATA step is carried out once for each observation.

Creating New Variables

When you create a new variable, you add another set of data values to your data set. As an example, see the session shown in **Screen 4.1**.

```
┌PROGRAM EDITOR───────────────────────────────────────────────────────┐
│Command ===>                                                          │
│                                                                      │
│00001 data profit;                                                    │
│00002    input year revenue expenses;                                 │
│00003    income=revenue-expenses;                                     │
│00004    cards;                                                       │
│00005 79 4976 2450                                                    │
│00006 80 5650 1050                                                    │
│00007 81 6280 1140                                                    │
│00008 run;                                                            │
│00009 proc print;                                                     │
│00010 run;                                                            │
│00011                                                                 │
│00012                                                                 │
│00013                                                                 │
│00014                                                                 │
│00015                                                                 │
│00016                                                                 │
│00017                                                                 │
│00018                                                                 │
│00019                                                                 │
│00020                                                                 │
│00021                                                         ─ZOOM─  │
└──────────────────────────────────────────────────────────────────────┘
```

Screen 4.1   Creating a New Variable

In data set PROFIT, you want to create a new variable named INCOME by subtracting the value of EXPENSES from the value of REVENUE. When you display the data set using PROC PRINT (**Screen 4.2**), INCOME is a variable in the data set.

```
┌OUTPUT────────────────────────────────────────────────────────┐
│Command ===>                                                   │
│                                                               │
│                           SAS                                 │
│                                                               │
│           OBS    YEAR    REVENUE    EXPENSES    INCOME         │
│                                                               │
│            1      79      4976       2450       2526          │
│            2      80      5650       1050       4600          │
│            3      81      6280       1140       5140          │
│                                                               │
│                                                               │
│                                                               │
│                                                               │
│                                                               │
│                                                               │
│                                                               │
│                                                               │
│                                                               │
│                                                        ▐ZOOM▌ │
└───────────────────────────────────────────────────────────────┘
```

Screen 4.2 Data Set PROFIT with Variable INCOME Added

To create a new variable:

1. Choose a name for the new variable; in this case, INCOME.
2. Figure out the formula necessary to create the variable. INCOME is calculated by subtracting expenses from revenue.
3. Write the formula as a SAS statement, putting the new variable name on the left side of the equal sign:

```
income=revenue-expenses;
```

This statement tells the SAS System to

- subtract the EXPENSES value from the REVENUE value for each observation in the data set.
- make the result the INCOME value for the observation.

SAS statements like the one above are called *assignment statements* because they assign values to variables. The form of the assignment statement is

resultvariable=*expression*;

SAS evaluates the expression on the right side of the equal sign and stores the result in the variable on the left.

Modifying Variables

You can also use an assignment statement to modify a variable that you already have in your data set. For example, suppose you want YEAR to be the full four-digit year instead of two digits. You can do that by adding 1900 to the current YEAR value:

four-digit year=two-digit year plus 1900.

The corresponding SAS statement is

```
year=year+1900;
```

This statement tells the SAS System to add 1900 to the old YEAR value in each observation and to make the result the new YEAR value for the observation.

Statements like the one above *look* as though you are saying that year equals year plus 1900, which is a confusing impossibility. But the equal sign here means "assign the value on the right to the variable on the left."

Table 4.1 shows the symbols to use in assignment statement calculations.

Table 4.1   Symbols Used in Assignment Statement Calculations

Symbol	Operation	Example	SAS Statement
**	powering	$Y=X^2$	Y=X**2;
*	multiplication	$A=B \times C$	A=B*C;
/	division	$G=H \div I$	G=H/I;
+	addition	$R=S+T$	R=S+T;
−	subtraction	$U=V-X$	U=V−X;

IF Statements

Sometimes you want the SAS System to carry out an action for certain observations in the data set, but not for all observations. For example, suppose you want to delete those sales representatives that sell computers. **Screen 4.3** shows how you can use an IF statement to do this.

When these statements are submitted to the SAS System, the following takes place. As the SAS System reads each observation, it checks the MACHINE value. If the MACHINE value is 'C', SAS carries out the DELETE statement and does not output the observation. When the MACHINE value is not 'C', SAS ignores the DELETE statement for that observation. The DELETE statement is described in more detail below.

Screen 4.4 is the OUTPUT window that results from printing the data set created by the DATA step in **Screen 4.3**.

```
┌PROGRAM EDITOR──────────────────────────────────────────────────────────┐
│Command ===>                                                            │
│                                                                        │
│00001 data sales;                                                       │
│00002    infile 'a:mydata.dat';                                         │
│00003    input salesrep $ 1-8 sales 10-15 region $ 19-23                │
│00004       machine $ 29-30;                                            │
│00005    if machine='C' then delete;                                    │
│00006 run;                                                              │
│00007 proc print;                                                       │
│00008 run;                                                              │
│00009                                                                   │
│00010                                                                   │
│00011                                                                   │
│00012                                                                   │
│00013                                                                   │
│00014                                                                   │
│00015                                                                   │
│00016                                                                   │
│00017                                                                   │
│00018                                                                   │
│00019                                                                   │
│00020                                                                   │
│00021                                                              ZOOM─┘
```

Screen 4.3   Using the IF Statement to Delete Specific Observations

```
┌OUTPUT──────────────────────────────────────────────────────────────────┐
│Command ===>                                                            │
│                                                                        │
│                              SAS                                       │
│                                                                        │
│         OBS    SALESREP    SALES    REGION    MACHINE                  │
│                                                                        │
│          1     Stafer       9664    east       SM                      │
│          2     Young       22969    east       SM                      │
│          3     Stride      27253    east       SM                      │
│          4     Curci       21531    west       SM                      │
│          5     Greco       18523    west       SM                      │
│          6     Ryan        32915    west       SM                      │
│          7     Tomas       42109    west       SM                      │
│          8     Moore       25718    south      SM                      │
│          9     Stelam      27634    south      SM                      │
│         10     Farlow      32719    north      SM                      │
│         11     Smith       38712    north      SM                      │
│                                                                        │
│                                                                  ZOOM─┘
```

Screen 4.4   OUTPUT Window Displaying PROC PRINT Output

IF statements have this form:

IF *condition* **THEN** *statement*;

For each observation, the IF condition is either *true* or *false*. For example, the IF condition MACHINE='C' is true for an observation where the MACHINE value is 'C'. It is false for observations where the MACHINE value is not 'C'. When the IF condition is true, the SAS System carries out the statement after the THEN.

The IF condition can be a simple comparison of a variable and a value:

```
if sales >25000 then output;
```

or a comparison of two variables

```
if month1 >month2 then trend='UP    ';
   else trend='DOWN';
```

The IF condition can involve several comparisons joined by ANDs and ORs:

```
if machine='C' and sales<30000 then put name;
```

```
if age<13 or age>65 then output;
```

Table 4.2 shows the operators you can use in IF conditions.

Table 4.2   Comparison Operators

Symbol	Abbreviation	Comparison
<	LT	less than
<=	LE	less than or equal to
>	GT	greater than
>=	GE	greater than or equal to
=	EQ	equal to
^=	NE	not equal to

DELETE Statements: Deleting Observations

When you want to discard certain observations, perhaps because you do not need them for your data analysis or because they contain invalid data, you can use the DELETE statement:

```
delete;
```

When this statement is carried out, SAS stops working on the current observation, does *not* add it to the SAS data set being created, and begins immediately on the next observation.

The DELETE statement normally appears as part of an IF statement:

```
if machine='C' then delete;
```

The IF condition (is the MACHINE value a 'C' ?) is checked for each observation. When an observation meets the condition, the SAS System carries out the DELETE statement: SAS stops working on the observation, does not add it to the data set, and returns immediately for the next observation.

When the IF condition is not true for an observation, SAS continues carrying out statements for the observation and adds it to the data set being created before returning for the next observation.

Subsetting IF Statements: Selecting Observations

In the previous example, you wanted only certain observations included in the data set being created: those sales representatives who did not sell computers. In the data set, the observations you wanted had a MACHINE value of 'SM', so you could have used a subsetting IF statement to include them:

```
if machine='SM';
```

This statement means, "If the MACHINE value for an observation is equal to 'SM', continue processing for that observation. If the MACHINE value for an observation is anything other than 'SM', stop processing statements for that observation and do not add the observation to the data set. Instead, return to the beginning of the DATA step for the next observation."

The subsetting IF statement has the same effect as the previous IF statement followed by a DELETE; it is just easier to write. These two statements have exactly the same effect on the sales data set:

```
if machine='SM';
```

and

```
if machine='C' then delete;
```

You might look at the subsetting IF statement as a gate that admits observations when the IF condition is true. Other observations cannot pass the gate.

SET Statements

Creating a SAS data set from another SAS data set   Until now, all the statements to reshape your data have been used in DATA steps that included an INPUT statement to describe the data. That is, all the input data have come from lines entered at a PC or from external files.

But your data can also come from a SAS data set that already exists. You can create another SAS data set using the observations from an existing SAS data set.

To do this, use the word SET in place of the INPUT and CARDS or INPUT and INFILE statements:

```
data reps;
   set sales;
```

The DATA statement tells the SAS System to begin creating a SAS data set, as usual. The SET statement tells the SAS System to get the data from the existing SAS data set SALES.

Usually, you use a SET statement in a DATA step when you want to modify the data in the existing SAS data set. For example, use the SAS statements shown in **Screen 4.5** to create a SAS data set containing sales representatives in the small machine group who have sales to date of more than $35,000.

```
┌PROGRAM EDITOR──────────────────────────────────────────────────┐
│Command ===>                                                     │
│                                                                 │
│00001 data toprep;                                               │
│00002    set sales;                                              │
│00003    if sales>35000 and machine ='SM';                       │
│00004 run;                                                       │
│00005 proc print;                                                │
│00006 run;                                                       │
│00007                                                            │
│00008                                                            │
│00009                                                            │
│00010                                                            │
│00011                                                            │
│00012                                                            │
│00013                                                            │
│00014                                                            │
│00015                                                            │
│00016                                                            │
│00017                                                            │
│00018                                                            │
│00019                                                            │
│00020                                                            │
│00021                                                  ──ZOOM──  │
└─────────────────────────────────────────────────────────────────┘
```

Screen 4.5   Using the SET Statement to Modify an Existing SAS Data Set

When you submit these statements to the SAS System, the new data set TOPREP contains just those observations from data set SALES whose MACHINE value is 'SM' and whose SALES value is greater than $35,000. The OUTPUT window (**Screen 4.6**) displays the PRINT procedure output, a listing of observations in the new data set.

```
┌OUTPUT─────────────────────────────────────────────────────────────────┐
│Command ===>                                                            │
│                                                                        │
│                                                                        │
│                                         SAS                            │
│                                                                        │
│              OBS    SALESREP    SALES    REGION    MACHINE             │
│                                                                        │
│               1      Tomas      42109    west        SM               │
│               2      Smith      38712    north       SM               │
│                                                                        │
│                                                                        │
│                                                                        │
│                                                                        │
│                                                                        │
│                                                                        │
│                                                                        │
│                                                                        │
│                                                                        │
│                                                                        │
│                                                                        │
│                                                                        │
│                                                                        │
│                                                                        │
│                                                                        │
│                                                                  ZOOM  │
└────────────────────────────────────────────────────────────────────────┘
```

Screen 4.6   OUTPUT Window Displaying PROC PRINT Output

This chapter describes some of the most commonly used SAS statements for shaping your data. These statements and others are described in detail in the *SAS Language Guide for Personal Computers, Release 6.03 Edition*.

48

Using SAS®
Procedures

DATA and PROC Steps

So far in this book you have learned to get your data into a SAS data set using:

- a DATA statement to begin creating the SAS data set
- an INPUT statement to describe the data to the SAS System
- optional SAS statements to modify the data
- an INFILE statement to point to the data, or
- a CARDS statement to signal the beginning of the data lines.

These statements together make up a *DATA step*, the part of a SAS session that creates a SAS data set.

Once you have created a SAS data set, you are ready to use SAS procedures to analyze and process that data set. SAS *procedures* are computer programs that read your SAS data set, perform various manipulations, and print the results of the computations.

For example, the PRINT procedure reads your SAS data set, arranges the data values in an easy-to-read form, and displays them. The MEANS procedure reads your SAS data set, computes the mean and other descriptive statistics, and prints those statistics. The FREQ procedure gives counts of your variable values in a frequency or crosstabulation table.

Some SAS procedures can also create SAS data sets containing the results of the computations. For example, the MEANS procedure can create a SAS data set containing means and other statistics.

The statements that ask the SAS System to run a procedure make up a PROC step, the part of a SAS session that processes and analyzes a SAS data set.

DATA and PROC steps get their names from the SAS statements DATA and PROC (short for PROCEDURE) that begin the steps. For example, **Screen 5.1** shows a SAS session that consists of a DATA step and a PROC step.

```
┌PROGRAM EDITOR─────────────────────────────────────────────────────┐
│Command ===>                                                        │
│                                                                    │
│00001 data class;                                                   │
│00002    input name $ test1 test2 test3;                            │
│00003    cards;                                                     │
│00004 john 90 86 88                                                 │
│00005 mary 100 98 89                                                │
│00006 ann 79 76 70                                                  │
│00007 bill 68 71 64                                                 │
│00008 tom 100 89 99                                                 │
│00009 run;                                                          │
│00010 proc means;                                                   │
│00011    var test1 test2 test3;                                     │
│00012 run;                                                          │
│00013                                                               │
│00014                                                               │
│00015                                                               │
│00016                                                               │
│00017                                                               │
│00018                                                               │
│00019                                                               │
│00020                                                               │
│00021                                                               │
│                                                            ─ZOOM───│
└────────────────────────────────────────────────────────────────────┘
```

Screen 5.1   A SAS Session Showing the DATA and PROC Steps

The DATA step (lines 00001 through 00009) begins with a DATA statement and creates a SAS data set named CLASS.

The PROC step (lines 00010 through 00012) begins with a PROC statement and processes the data set.

How to Combine DATA and PROC Steps to Use the SAS System

You use the SAS System by stringing together DATA steps and PROC steps.

Simple SAS sessions, like the ones you have seen so far in this book, usually consist of a DATA step followed by one or more PROC steps.

Often, though, you want to work with more than one data set in a SAS session. For example, consider the sales data set in the first part of this book. You might want to create a second data set containing last year's sales figures for the sales representatives. Then, after analyzing each data set separately, you might want to combine the data sets to form a third one.

DATA steps and PROC steps do not have to come in any special order. You can start with a DATA or PROC step, then use a PROC step, another PROC step, then a DATA step, and so on.

Once you create a SAS data set in a SAS session, you can use that data set at any point in the session.

How to Use PROC Steps to Get Answers

The PROC step always begins with a PROC statement giving the name of the SAS procedure you want to run. For example, if you want to run the PRINT procedure, you begin the PROC step with the statement

```
proc print;
```

SAS procedures for processing data are alike in that you can tell the procedure:

- what data set you want processed
- whether you want the data set processed in subsets
- which variables you want processed.

The Most Common Situation

Most SAS procedures automatically handle the most common situation, where you want

- to process the most recently created SAS data set
- all the variables processed (or all the numeric variables, for a computational procedure)
- the entire data set processed at once, rather than in subsets.

Since the SAS System handles this situation automatically, most of the time your PROC step need only include a PROC statement giving the name of the procedure you want to run followed by a RUN statement. For example, these statements

```
proc print;
run;
```

are a PROC step that asks the SAS System to read the most recently created SAS data set, arrange all the variables in an easy-to-read form, and display them.

Combining the sales information DATA step with this PROC step gives us the simple SAS session shown in **Screen 5.2**.

The PROC PRINT statement in the session shown in **Screen 5.2** asks for the most common situation: you want to process the most recently created SAS data set, SALES; you want all variables in the data set displayed; and you want the data set processed all at once, rather than in subsets.

The output from these two steps is shown in **Screen 5.3**.

```
┌PROGRAM EDITOR─────────────────────────────────────────────────
Command ===>

00001 data sales;
00002    infile 'a:mydata.dat';
00003    input salesrep $ 1-8 sales 10-15 region $ 19-23
00004           machine $ 29-30;
00005 run;
00006 proc print;
00007 run;
00008
00009
00010
00011
00012
00013
00014
00015
00016
00017
00018
00019
00020
00021
                                                         ─ZOOM─
```

Screen 5.2   A Simple SAS Session

```
┌OUTPUT─────────────────────────────────────────────────────────
Command ===>

                              SAS                              1

        OBS    SALESREP    SALES    REGION    MACHINE

          1    Stafer       9664    east        SM
          2    Young       22969    east        SM
          3    Stride      27253    east        SM
          4    Topin       86432    east        C
          5    Spark       99210    east        C
          6    Vetter      38928    west        C
          7    Curci       21531    west        SM
          8    Marco       79345    west        C
          9    Greco       18523    west        SM
         10    Ryan        32915    west        SM
         11    Tomas       42109    west        SM
         12    Thalman     94320    south       C
         13    Moore       25718    south       SM
         14    Allen       64700    south       C
         15    Stelam      27634    south       SM
         16    Farlow      32719    north       SM
         17    Smith       38712    north       SM
                                                  ZOOM
```

Screen 5.3   Output Generated by a Simple SAS Session

SAS procedures sometimes do require additional statements to give the procedure more information about what you want. For example, the PLOT procedure requires a PLOT statement to tell the SAS System what variable you want on the vertical axis and what variable on the horizontal axis:

```
proc plot;
   plot weight*price;
run;
```

This PROC step asks the SAS System to read the most recently created SAS data set and plot the variable WEIGHT on the vertical axis versus the variable PRICE on the horizontal axis. (The first variable mentioned in the PLOT statement goes on the vertical axis; the second variable mentioned is used on the horizontal axis.)

Telling the PROC What Data Set You Want Processed

If you want the procedure to use the last data set you created or if you have created only one data set, your PROC statement need give only the procedure name:

```
proc print;
run;
```

When you want the procedure to use a data set that is not the one most recently created, when you want to process a permanently stored SAS data set that was created in another SAS session, or when several data sets are created in the session and you want to minimize confusion, specify the name of the SAS data set you want processed after the word DATA followed by an equal sign:

```
proc print data=sales;
run;
```

The PROC PRINT statement tells the SAS System to execute the PRINT procedure using the data set SALES.

Telling the PROC What Variables You Want Processed

If you want the procedure to use all the variables in your SAS data set, you need only the PROC statement because the procedure automatically uses all of the variables. (Some procedures automatically use all the numeric variables.)

But if you want to analyze only certain variables, you can use the VAR (short for VARIABLES) statement to give the names of these variables:

```
proc print;
   var salesrep sales;
run;
```

The PROC statement tells the SAS System that you want to run the PRINT procedure on the most recently created data set. The VAR statement tells the SAS System that only the variables SALESREP and SALES are to be displayed.

Do You Want Your Data Processed in Groups?

If you want your entire data set processed at once, the SAS System automatically handles it that way.

Often however, you want your data processed in groups. In the sales data set, the variable MACHINE identifies the product line sold by each representative.

You might want to run PROC MEANS first for the sales representatives who sell computers, then for those who sell small machines (since 'C' is "lower" than 'SM').

If you want the SAS System to process data in groups, your data set must be arranged in groups. You use a BY statement to tell SAS procedures how the data are to be processed. In the BY statement, give the variable (or variables) that define the group.

For example, to run the MEANS procedure first for computers, then for small machines, you give the variable MACHINE in the BY statement as shown in **Screen 5.4**. Since the data are not sorted in that order, first use PROC SORT with a BY statement, then use PROC MEANS with a BY statement.

The statements shown in **Screen 5.4** ask the SAS System to

- run the procedure SORT on the data set SALES, grouping by values of MACHINE
- run the procedure MEANS on the most recently created data set (the sorted data set from the PROC SORT step)
- use all numeric variables for analysis
- run the procedure first on the observations having a 'C' value for MACHINE, then on the observations having the value 'SM'.

Screen 5.5 shows the output produced by the statements.

The next chapter gives a brief description of four commonly used SAS procedures: SORT, PRINT, FREQ, and MEANS. For information about other procedures in base SAS software, read the procedure descriptions in the *SAS Procedures Guide, Release 6.03 Edition*.

```
┌PROGRAM EDITOR──────────────────────────────────────────────────────────────
│Command ===>
│
│00001 proc sort data=sales;
│00002    by machine;
│00003 run;
│00004 proc means;
│00005    by machine;
│00006 run;
│00007
│00008
│00009
│00010
│00011
│00012
│00013
│00014
│00015
│00016
│00017
│00018
│00019
│00020
│00021                                                                    ┌ZOOM┐
```

Screen 5.4   Processing the Data in Groups

```
┌OUTPUT──────────────────────────────────────────────────────────────────────
│Command ===>
│
│                                    SAS                                      3
│
│      Analysis Variable : SALES
│
│
│   ──────────────────────────────── MACHINE=C ───────────────────────────────
│
│
│      N Obs   N      Minimum        Maximum          Mean        Std Dev
│      ────────────────────────────────────────────────────────────────
│          7   7     38928.00       99210.00      80021.29      21730.18
│      ────────────────────────────────────────────────────────────────
│
│   ──────────────────────────────── MACHINE=SM ──────────────────────────────
│
│
│      N Obs   N      Minimum        Maximum          Mean        Std Dev
│      ────────────────────────────────────────────────────────────────
│         11  11      9664.00       42109.00      27249.73       9236.48
│      ────────────────────────────────────────────────────────────────
│                                                                      ┌ZOOM┐
```

Screen 5.5   Output Produced from the Grouped Data

Chapter 6

Rearranging, Displaying, and Summarizing Your Data

Now that you have learned how SAS procedures work and how they relate to your data, you need to look at some of the basic SAS procedures that are used most often to rearrange, display, and summarize data.

Once you learn how to use these procedures, you can easily use other procedures in the SAS System. You just need to know what you want to do with your data. Then you find a SAS procedure that performs that analysis and learn the statements you need to use the procedure with your data.

This chapter describes four commonly used SAS procedures—SORT, PRINT, FREQ, and MEANS. For descriptions of other procedures in base SAS software, see the *SAS Procedures Guide, Release 6.03 Edition.*

USING PROC SORT TO REARRANGE YOUR DATA

Since data are often recorded in random order, they are usually still in this order when you are ready to analyze them using the SAS System. United States rainfall data may have Alabama's data following Wyoming's information; Mr. Zimmerman's tax information may come before Ms. Adams'; and our sales information had computer and small business sales representatives intermixed.

When Do You Need to Sort Your Data?

The order of the observations does not matter for much of the statistical processing you will do. For example, the mean January sales is the same number no matter what the order of observations.

Often, however, you do want the observations arranged in some definite order. For example, to check the United States rainfall data, you might want to print them by state: Alabama followed by Alaska, and so on. You might want to list the tax information in alphabetical order by name. Or you might want to look at your sales representatives by machine, computers and then small machines.

The SAS System often needs the observations in a data set to be in some definite order. For example, to display an alphabetical listing of sales representatives, the data would need to be sorted in alphabetical order by sales representative. As we discussed in "Using SAS Procedures," a data set must be sorted before you can use a BY statement to process it.

What Is Sorting?

Sorting is rearranging the observations in your data set into an order determined by the values of one or more variables.

For example, suppose you wanted the sales information in order by sales representative. In that case, you would arrange the data alphabetically by last name. Or, you might want the sales information in ascending order of year-to-date sales so that the sales representative with the smallest total sales comes first.

In both these cases, you are sorting by one variable: the first sort is by last name, and the second is by year-to-date sales.

A different situation would be sorting questionnaires from a survey. First you put them in order by state. Next, for each state, you put the questionnaires in order by city. Finally, you alphabetize each city's questionnaires by the respondent's last name.

In this case, you are sorting by three variables—the state, the city, and the respondent's name.

How to Use PROC SORT

To sort your data, use a PROC SORT statement followed by a BY statement that gives the variables by which you want to sort the data set.

For example, these statements sort the sales information data set by SALESREP, the representatives' last names:

```
proc sort data=sales;
   by salesrep;
run;
```

If you want to sort a data set named SURVEY by state, then by city within state, and finally by name within city, you would use these statements:

```
proc sort data=survey;
   by state city name;
run;
```

Getting sorted and unsorted versions of your data The SAS System normally reads the data set identified by DATA= in the PROC SORT statement (or the most recently created data set if DATA= is not used). SAS rearranges this data set in the order of the variables in the BY statement and stores the rearranged data with the same data set name. The unsorted version of the data set disappears.

If you want to keep the unsorted version of the data set, specify OUT= in the PROC SORT statement to create another data set containing the sorted data:

```
proc sort data=sales out=ordered;
   by machine;
run;
```

Now you have two data sets, SALES and ORDERED. Data set ORDERED contains the same observations as data set SALES, but they are sorted by the values of the variable MACHINE.

PROC SORT Output

PROC SORT does not produce any procedure output, although it does display information on the SAS log telling how much time it used and how many observations the sorted data set contains (**Screen 6.1**).

```
LOG
Command ===>

   23    proc sort data=sales out=ordered;
   24       by machine;
   25    run;
NOTE: The data set WORK.ORDERED has 18 observations and 4 variables.
NOTE: The PROCEDURE SORT used 13.00 seconds.



                                                              ZOOM
```

Screen 6.1 SAS Log Resulting from PROC SORT

USING PROC PRINT TO DISPLAY YOUR DATA

The natural first step after getting your data into a SAS data set is to display it.

You want to verify that the data were read correctly. You want to check for data entry errors. And you may see an obvious mistake that will alert you to other, not-so-obvious problems.

Displaying your data also gives you a handy reference to the data values them-selves. The display is useful even when you are really interested in summarizing the data rather than looking at individual values.

How to Display Your Data

After you have used a DATA step to get your data values into a SAS data set, you can display the data in an easy-to-read form with the statements

```
proc print;
run;
```

Screen 6.2 shows the SAS statements needed to display the sales data. **Screen 6.3** shows the first page of the results.

Using just the PROC PRINT statement displays the most recently created SAS data set. If you want to display some other data set, you can specify DATA= in the PROC PRINT statement:

```
proc print data=old;
run;
```

```
┌PROGRAM EDITOR──────────────────────────────────────────────────────┐
│Command ===>                                                         │
│                                                                     │
│00001 data sales;                                                    │
│00002    infile 'a:mydata.dat';                                      │
│00003    input salesrep $ 1-8 sales 10-15 region $ 19-23             │
│00004          machine $ 29-30;                                      │
│00005 run;                                                           │
│00006 proc print;                                                    │
│00007 run;                                                           │
│00008                                                                │
│00009                                                                │
│00010                                                                │
│00011                                                                │
│00012                                                                │
│00013                                                                │
│00014                                                                │
│00015                                                                │
│00016                                                                │
│00017                                                                │
│00018                                                                │
│00019                                                                │
│00020                                                                │
│00021                                                            ZOOM│
└─────────────────────────────────────────────────────────────────────┘
```

Screen 6.2   SAS Statements Needed to Display Sales Data

```
┌OUTPUT──────────────────────────────────────────────────────────────┐
│Command ===>                                                         │
│                                                                     │
│                              SAS                              1      │
│                                                                     │
│          OBS    SALESREP    SALES    REGION    MACHINE              │
│                                                                     │
│            1    Stafer       9664    east        SM                 │
│            2    Young       22969    east        SM                 │
│            3    Stride      27253    east        SM                 │
│            4    Topin       86432    east        C                  │
│            5    Spark       99210    east        C                  │
│            6    Vetter      38928    west        C                  │
│            7    Curci       21531    west        SM                 │
│            8    Marco       79345    west        C                  │
│            9    Greco       18523    west        SM                 │
│           10    Ryan        32915    west        SM                 │
│           11    Tomas       42109    west        SM                 │
│           12    Thalman     94320    south       C                  │
│           13    Moore       25718    south       SM                 │
│           14    Allen       64700    south       C                  │
│           15    Stelam      27634    south       SM                 │
│           16    Farlow      32719    north       SM                 │
│           17    Smith       38712    north       SM            ZOOM │
└─────────────────────────────────────────────────────────────────────┘
```

Screen 6.3   Display of SAS Data Set SALES

Adding Titles and Footnotes to Your Report

You can put up to 10 titles and 10 footnotes on the report. The titles and footnotes that appear on any SAS procedure output come from the TITLES and FOOTNOTES windows of the SAS Display Manager System.

You can go directly to these windows to define titles and footnotes for your report. Or you can use TITLE or FOOTNOTE statements and the SAS System adds the titles and footnotes to the windows automatically.

For example, the PROC step shown in **Screen 6.4** has two TITLE statements added. The output has titles on the first and third lines and is shown in **Screen 6.5** and **Screen 6.6**.

The titles you entered in the step shown in **Screen 6.4** are automatically placed in the TITLES window in the SAS Display Manager System.

```
┌PROGRAM EDITOR───────────────────────────────────────────────────┐
│Command ===>                                                     │
│                                                                 │
│00001 proc print data=sales;                                    │
│00002     title 'Sales Representatives';                        │
│00003     title3 'XYZ Manufacturing Company';                   │
│00004 run;                                                       │
│00005                                                            │
│00006                                                            │
│00007                                                            │
│00008                                                            │
│00009                                                            │
│00010                                                            │
│00011                                                            │
│00012                                                            │
│00013                                                            │
│00014                                                            │
│00015                                                            │
│00016                                                            │
│00017                                                            │
│00018                                                            │
│00019                                                            │
│00020                                                            │
│00021                                                            │
│                                                          ─ZOOM─ │
└─────────────────────────────────────────────────────────────────┘
```

Screen 6.4   PROC Step with TITLE Statements

```
┌OUTPUT─────────────────────────────────────────────────────────────┐
│Command ===>                                                        │
│                          °                                         │
│                                                                    │
│                         Sales Representatives                      │
│                                                                    │
│                      XYZ Manufacturing Company                     │
│                                                                    │
│            OBS    SALESREP    SALES    REGION    MACHINE           │
│                                                                    │
│             1     Stafer       9664    east        SM              │
│             2     Young       22969    east        SM              │
│             3     Stride      27253    east        SM              │
│             4     Topin       86432    east        C               │
│             5     Spark       99210    east        C               │
│             6     Vetter      38928    west        C               │
│             7     Curci       21531    west        SM              │
│             8     Marco       79345    west        C               │
│             9     Greco       18523    west        SM              │
│            10     Ryan        32915    west        SM              │
│            11     Tomas       42109    west        SM              │
│            12     Thalman     94320    south       C               │
│            13     Moore       25718    south       SM              │
│            14     Allen       64700    south       C               │
│            15     Stelam      27634    south       SM   ┌────┐     │
│                                                         │ZOOM│     │
└─────────────────────────────────────────────────────────────────┘
```

Screen 6.5   Output with Titles

```
┌OUTPUT─────────────────────────────────────────────────────────────┐
│Command ===>                                                        │
│                                                                    │
│                                                                    │
│                         Sales Representatives                      │
│                                                                    │
│                      XYZ Manufacturing Company                     │
│                                                                    │
│            OBS    SALESREP    SALES    REGION    MACHINE           │
│                                                                    │
│            16     Farlow      32719    north       SM              │
│            17     Smith       38712    north       SM              │
│            18     Wilson      97214    north       C               │
│                                                                    │
│                                                                    │
│                                                                    │
│                                                                    │
│                                                                    │
│                                                                    │
│                                                                    │
│                                                                    │
│                                                                    │
│                                                                    │
│                                                        ┌────┐      │
│                                                        │ZOOM│      │
└─────────────────────────────────────────────────────────────────┘
```

Screen 6.6   Continuation of Output with Titles

To view the TITLES window (**Screen 6.7**), hold down the Ctrl key and press T (or enter the TITLES command and press ENTER). The TITLE statements you entered in the previous step have been inserted in the window. Note that titles entered in the window do not require single quotes.

If you want to modify or add titles, you can do it directly in the window. After you add or change titles, enter END on the command line and press ENTER. The titles and footnotes are submitted to the SAS System and the TITLES window disappears from the screen. The titles or footnotes appear on subsequent procedure output.

For footnotes, use FOOTNOTE statements or the FOOTNOTES window just as for titles. Both FOOTNOTES and TITLES windows are described in detail in the *SAS Language Guide for Personal Computers, Release 6.03 Edition*.

```
┌TITLES───────────────────────────────────────────────────────────────────┐
│Command ===>                                                              │
│                                                                          │
│Title Description                                                         │
│    1   Sales Representatives                                             │
│    2                                                                     │
│    3   XYZ Manufacturing Company                                        │
│    4                                                                     │
│    5                                                                     │
│    6                                                                     │
│    7                                                                     │
│    8                                                                     │
│    9                                                                     │
│   10                                                                     │
│                                                                          │
│                                                                          │
│                                                                          │
│                                                                          │
│                                                                          │
│                                                                    ZOOM  │
└──────────────────────────────────────────────────────────────────────────┘
```

Screen 6.7   The TITLES Window

Displaying Groups of Your Data

When your data include several groups, you can display a separate list for each group. For example, the statements shown in **Screen 6.8** sort the SALES data set by MACHINE, then display the sales information for sales representatives who sell computers (MACHINE=C) and then for sales representatives of small machines (MACHINE=SM). The output is shown in **Screen 6.9** and **Screen 6.10**. The titles you entered earlier are still in effect and are displayed on the output.

```
PROGRAM EDITOR
Command ===>

00001 proc sort data=sales;
00002    by machine;
00003 run;
00004 proc print;
00005    by machine;
00006 run;
00007
00008
00009
00010
00011
00012
00013
00014
00015
00016
00017
00018
00019
00020
00021
                                                              ZOOM
```

Screen 6.8   SAS Statements to Sort SALES Data Set

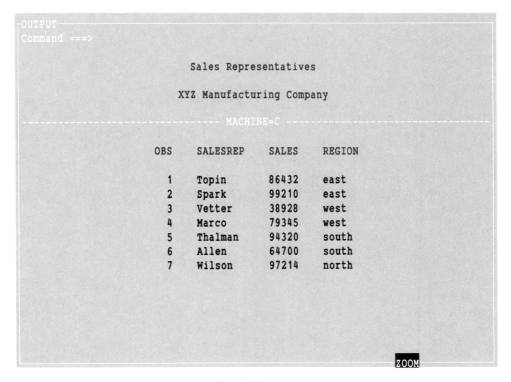

Screen 6.9   SALES Data Set Displayed by Groups

```
┌─OUTPUT────────────────────────────────────────────────────────────────┐
│Command ===>                                                            │
│                                                                        │
│                                                                        │
│                        Sales Representatives                           │
│                                                                        │
│                     XYZ Manufacturing Company                          │
│                                                                        │
│ ──────────────────────────── MACHINE=SM ────────────────────────────── │
│                                                                        │
│              OBS     SALESREP    SALES    REGION                       │
│                                                                        │
│               8      Stafer       9664    east                         │
│               9      Young       22969    east                         │
│              10      Stride      27253    east                         │
│              11      Curci       21531    west                         │
│              12      Greco       18523    west                         │
│              13      Ryan        32915    west                         │
│              14      Tomas       42109    west                         │
│              15      Moore       25718    south                        │
│              16      Stelam      27634    south                        │
│              17      Farlow      32719    north                        │
│              18      Smith       38712    north                        │
│                                                                        │
│                                                               ┌────┐   │
│                                                               │ZOOM│   │
│                                                               └────┘   │
└────────────────────────────────────────────────────────────────────────┘
```

Screen 6.10   Continuation of Output

Listing the Variables in the Order You Want

So far, you have displayed all the variables in the same order they appeared in the data set.

You can select certain variables to be displayed and ask that they appear in a certain order by using the VAR (short for VARIABLES) statement. For example, the statements shown in **Screen 6.11** ask the SAS System to display just the REGION, SALESREP, and SALES variables in that order. The first "page" of output is shown in **Screen 6.12**.

The VAR statement follows the PROC statement and comes before the RUN statement in a PROC step. After the word VAR just list the names of the variables you want displayed in the order you want them.

```
┌PROGRAM EDITOR──────────────────────────────────────────────────────
Command ===>

00001 proc print data=sales;
00002    var region salesrep sales;
00003 run;
00004
00005
00006
00007
00008
00009
00010
00011
00012
00013
00014
00015
00016
00017
00018
00019
00020
00021
                                                              ──ZOOM──
```

Screen 6.11   SAS Statements to Display Certain Variables

```
┌OUTPUT──────────────────────────────────────────────────────────────
Command ===>


                      Sales Representatives

                   XYZ Manufacturing Company

              OBS    REGION    SALESREP    SALES

                1    east      Stafer       9664
                2    east      Young       22969
                3    east      Stride      27253
                4    east      Topin       86432
                5    east      Spark       99210
                6    west      Vetter      38928
                7    west      Curci       21531
                8    west      Marco       79345
                9    west      Greco       18523
               10    west      Ryan        32915
               11    west      Tomas       42109
               12    south     Thalman     94320
               13    south     Moore       25718
               14    south     Allen       64700
               15    south     Stelam      27634
                                                     ZOOM
```

Screen 6.12   Display of Certain Variables

Omitting the OBS Column

In the previous examples, output from PROC PRINT has included a column labeled OBS that gives the observation number. You can omit this column from the report by using an ID statement to give the name of a variable you want to appear first in the listing.

For example, the statements shown in **Screen 6.13** include an ID statement to specify that REGION should appear first in the report. The VAR statement gives the other variables you want to appear. **Screen 6.14** shows the first page of the resulting report.

```
┌PROGRAM EDITOR─────────────────────────────────────────────────────
│Command ===>
│
│00001 proc print data=sales;
│00002    id region;
│00003    var salesrep sales;
│00004 run;
│00005
│00006
│00007
│00008
│00009
│00010
│00011
│00012
│00013
│00014
│00015
│00016
│00017
│00018
│00019
│00020
│00021
│                                                              ──ZOOM──
```

Screen 6.13   Using an ID Statement to Specify REGION as the First Variable in Display

```
 OUTPUT
 Command ===>


                        Sales Representatives

                     XYZ Manufacturing Company

               REGION      SALESREP      SALES

                east       Stafer         9664
                east       Young         22969
                east       Stride        27253
                east       Topin         86432
                east       Spark         99210
                west       Vetter        38928
                west       Curci         21531
                west       Marco         79345
                west       Greco         18523
                west       Ryan          32915
                west       Tomas         42109
                south      Thalman       94320
                south      Moore         25718
                south      Allen         64700
                south      Stelam        27634
                                                        ZOOM
```

Screen 6.14   Display with REGION as the First Variable

Totaling Variable Values

If you have a numeric variable in your data set that you want totaled, you can use the SUM statement to indicate which variable you want to have a cumulative total.

For example, suppose you want to sum the year-to-date sales and add the sums to the report shown in **Screen 6.14**. Just add the SUM statement to the PROC step and give the name of the variable you want totaled. The variable need not appear in the VAR statement if it appears in the SUM statement. The statements you need are shown in **Screen 6.15**. The results are shown in **Screen 6.16** and **Screen 6.17**.

The SUM statement follows the PROC statement and comes before the RUN statement. Its order among the other PROC step statements is not important. After the word SUM, just list the names of any variables you want totaled.

```
┌PROGRAM EDITOR────────────────────────────────────────────────────────────┐
│Command ===>                                                               │
│                                                                           │
│00001 proc print data=sales;                                              │
│00002    id region;                                                        │
│00003    var salesrep;                                                     │
│00004    sum sales;                                                        │
│00005 run;                                                                 │
│00006                                                                      │
│00007                                                                      │
│00008                                                                      │
│00009                                                                      │
│00010                                                                      │
│00011                                                                      │
│00012                                                                      │
│00013                                                                      │
│00014                                                                      │
│00015                                                                      │
│00016                                                                      │
│00017                                                                      │
│00018                                                                      │
│00019                                                                      │
│00020                                                                      │
│00021                                                             ─ZOOM─   │
└───────────────────────────────────────────────────────────────────────────┘
```

Screen 6.15   SUM Statement Added to the PROC Step to Total SALES Variable

```
┌OUTPUT──────────────────────────────────────────────────────────────────┐
│Command ===>                                                             │
│                                                                         │
│                      Sales Representatives                              │
│                                                                         │
│                   XYZ Manufacturing Company                             │
│                                                                         │
│            REGION      SALESREP      SALES                              │
│                                                                         │
│            east        Stafer         9664                             │
│            east        Young         22969                             │
│            east        Stride        27253                             │
│            east        Topin         86432                             │
│            east        Spark         99210                             │
│            west        Vetter        38928                             │
│            west        Curci         21531                             │
│            west        Marco         79345                             │
│            west        Greco         18523                             │
│            west        Ryan          32915                             │
│            west        Tomas         42109                             │
│            south       Thalman       94320                             │
│            south       Moore         25718                             │
│            south       Allen         64700                             │
│            south       Stelam        27634                   ZOOM      │
└─────────────────────────────────────────────────────────────────────────┘
```

Screen 6.16   Display of SALES Data Set with Variable Totaled

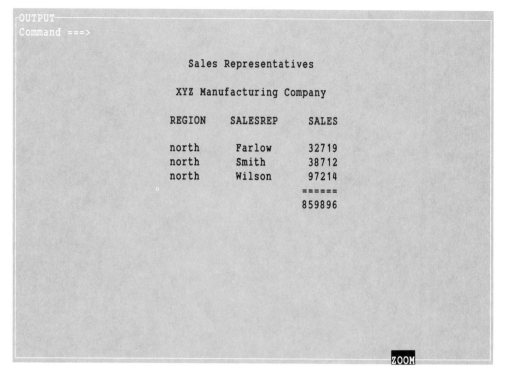

┌OUTPUT─
Command ===>

Sales Representatives

XYZ Manufacturing Company

REGION   SALESREP   SALES

north   Farlow   32719
north   Smith   38712
north   Wilson   97214
                          ======
                          859896

Screen 6.17   Continuation of Display

Totals for Subsets

If you use a SUM statement in a PROC step that has a BY statement, the SAS System gives you totals for each subgroup specified by the BY statement. (Make sure the data set being processed is sorted in order of the BY variable.)

For example, to sort the data set by region and then get the total sales for each region, use the statements shown in **Screen 6.18**. The first and last pages of the resulting report are shown in **Screen 6.19** and **Screen 6.20**.

Fancier Reports

These examples are simple reports, easily produced using the PRINT procedure. The reports that you can display with PROC PRINT are limited only by the data set you can build. And you have already learned some ways to subset your data set and transform and build new variables. Now think of ways to combine a DATA step with PROC PRINT to produce other kinds of reports.

```
┌PROGRAM EDITOR──────────────────────────────────────────────────┐
│Command ===>                                                     │
│                                                                 │
│00001 proc sort data=sales;                                      │
│00002    by region;                                              │
│00003 run;                                                       │
│00004 proc print;                                                │
│00005    by region;                                              │
│00006    id salesrep;                                            │
│00007    sum sales;                                              │
│00008 run;                                                       │
│00009                                                            │
│00010                                                            │
│00011                                                            │
│00012                                                            │
│00013                                                            │
│00014                                                            │
│00015                                                            │
│00016                                                            │
│00017                                                            │
│00018                                                            │
│00019                                                            │
│00020                                                            │
│00021                                                     ZOOM   │
└─────────────────────────────────────────────────────────────────┘
```

Screen 6.18   Sorting the Data Set by Region and Determining Total Sales by Region

```
┌OUTPUT──────────────────────────────────────────────────────────┐
│Command ===>                                                     │
│                                                                 │
│                     Sales Representatives                       │
│                                                                 │
│                   XYZ Manufacturing Company                     │
│                                                                 │
│ ----------------------------- REGION=east --------------------- │
│                                                                 │
│              SALESREP     SALES     MACHINE                      │
│                                                                 │
│              Stafer        9664       SM                        │
│              Young        22969       SM                        │
│              Stride       27253       SM                        │
│              Topin        86432       C                         │
│              Spark        99210       C                         │
│                          ------                                 │
│              REGION      245528                                 │
│                                                                 │
│                                                                 │
│                                                                 │
│                                                          ZOOM   │
└─────────────────────────────────────────────────────────────────┘
```

Screen 6.19   Display Showing Total Sales by Region

```
┌OUTPUT─────────────────────────────────────────────────────────────────
│Command ===>

                    Sales Representatives

                  XYZ Manufacturing Company

        ─────────────────────── REGION=west ───────────────────────────

                 SALESREP      SALES     MACHINE

                  Vetter       38928       C
                  Curci        21531       SM
                  Marco        79345       C
                  Greco        18523       SM
                  Ryan         32915       SM
                  Tomas        42109       SM
                               ──────
                  REGION       233351
                               ======
                               859896


                                                              ┌────┐
                                                              │ZOOM│
                                                              └────┘
```

Screen 6.20   Continuation of Display Showing Total Sales by Region

USING PROC FREQ FOR FREQUENCIES AND CROSSTABULATIONS

Frequency tables are a good way to summarize your data. They show the distribution of a variable's values; you see at a glance how many observations in the data set have a given value. For example, say you want to know how many sales representatives you have in each region—east, north, south, and west.

Screen 6.21 shows the statements you use to find how many observations have each REGION value. The result is shown in **Screen 6.22**.

```
┌PROGRAM EDITOR──────────────────────────────────────────────────────
Command ===>

00001 proc freq data=sales;
00002    tables region;
00003 run;
00004
00005
00006
00007
00008
00009
00010
00011
00012
00013
00014
00015
00016
00017
00018
00019
00020
00021                                                            ZOOM
```

Screen 6.21   SAS Statements to Determine Observations per Region

```
┌OUTPUT───────────────────────────────────────────────────────────────
Command ===>




                                      Cumulative  Cumulative
        REGION    Frequency   Percent   Frequency    Percent
        ---------------------------------------------------------
        east          5        27.8         5         27.8
        north         3        16.7         8         44.4
        south         4        22.2        12         66.7
        west          6        33.3        18        100.0






                                                           ZOOM
```

Screen 6.22   Frequency Table by Region

You can break the data down further with crosstabulation tables, which show the joint distribution of two variables' values. For example, say you want to know how many sales representatives who sell each machine type are in each region. You use the two variables REGION and MACHINE in the TABLES statement to find how many observations have a REGION value of 'east' and a MACHINE value of 'C', and so on (**Screen 6.23**). The resulting crosstabulation is shown in **Screen 6.24**.

Crosstabulation tables can also show the distribution of values for three or more variables.

```
┌PROGRAM EDITOR─────────────────────────────────────────────────────────┐
│Command ===>                    ·                                       │
│                                                                        │
│00001 proc freq data=sales;                                             │
│00002    tables machine*region;                                         │
│00003 run;                                                              │
│00004                                                                   │
│00005                                                                   │
│00006                                                                   │
│00007                                                                   │
│00008                                                                   │
│00009                                                                   │
│00010                                                                   │
│00011                                                                   │
│00012                                                                   │
│00013                                                                   │
│00014                                                                   │
│00015                                                                   │
│00016                                                                   │
│00017                                                                   │
│00018                                                                   │
│00019                                                                   │
│00020                                                                   │
│00021                                                              ZOOM─┘
```

Screen 6.23   SAS Statements to Determine Representatives Selling Each Machine by Region

```
┌─OUTPUT────────────────────────────────────────────────────────────────┐
│ Command ===>                                                            │
│                                                                         │
│                                    SAS                                  │
│                                                                         │
│                          TABLE OF MACHINE BY REGION                     │
│                                                                         │
│              MACHINE      REGION                                        │
│                                                                         │
│              Frequency│                                                 │
│              Percent  │                                                 │
│              Row Pct  │                                                 │
│              Col Pct  │east    │north   │south   │west    │ Total       │
│              ─────────┼────────┼────────┼────────┼────────┤            │
│              C        │    2 │     1 │     2 │     2 │     7           │
│                       │ 11.11 │  5.56 │ 11.11 │ 11.11 │ 38.89           │
│                       │ 28.57 │ 14.29 │ 28.57 │ 28.57 │                 │
│                       │ 40.00 │ 33.33 │ 50.00 │ 33.33 │                 │
│              ─────────┼────────┼────────┼────────┼────────┤            │
│              Total        5       3       4       6       18            │
│                         27.78   16.67   22.22   33.33  100.00           │
│              (Continued)                                                │
│                                                                  ▮ZOOM  │
└─────────────────────────────────────────────────────────────────────────┘
```

Screen 6.24   Crosstabulation Table of Machine by Region

For What Kinds of Variables Are Frequencies Useful?

Frequencies and crosstabulations are useful mainly for *discrete* variables; that is, those having several distinct values. For example, the variable REGION in our example has four values and MACHINE has two values. You can get useful information by determining frequencies for REGION and MACHINE.

However, variables like SALES have many values. For these continuous variables, statistics such as the mean and standard deviation are more useful.

Another benefit of frequencies and crosstabulations is that you can summarize character variables. However, only numeric variables can be summarized by the mean and standard deviation.

How to Get Frequencies

To get frequency tables for all the variables in the most recently created data set, just use a PROC FREQ and a RUN statement:

```
proc freq;
run;
```

If you want to use another data set, use DATA= in the PROC FREQ statement:

```
proc freq data=old;
run;
```

There is little purpose in getting frequency tables for variables like SALESREP that have many values. Thus, you will usually ask SAS to print frequencies for only selected variables in your data set. Give their names in a TABLES statement after the PROC FREQ statement, as shown in **Screen 6.25**. The resulting tables are shown in **Screen 6.26**.

```
┌PROGRAM EDITOR─────────────────────────────────────────────────────
Command ===>

00001 proc freq data=sales;
00002    tables machine region;
00003 run;
00004
00005
00006
00007
00008
00009
00010
00011
00012
00013
00014
00015
00016
00017
00018
00019
00020
00021                                                              ZOOM
```

Screen 6.25   SAS Statements for Two One-Way Frequency Tables

```
┌OUTPUT──────────────────────────────────────────────────────────────
Command ===>


                              SAS

                                       Cumulative  Cumulative
         MACHINE   Frequency   Percent   Frequency   Percent
         ------------------------------------------------------
         C              7       38.9          7       38.9
         SM            11       61.1         18      100.0




                                       Cumulative  Cumulative
         REGION    Frequency   Percent   Frequency   Percent
         ------------------------------------------------------
         east           5       27.8          5       27.8
         north          3       16.7          8       44.4
         south          4       22.2         12       66.7
         west           6       33.3         18      100.0



                                                                 ZOOM
```

Screen 6.26   Frequency Table of Machines and Regions

How to Get Crosstabulation Tables

To get a crosstabulation table, follow the PROC FREQ statement with a TABLES statement. Put first the variable you want down the side of the table, then an asterisk (*), then the variable you want across the top:

```
proc freq;
   tables machine*region;
run;
```

You can ask for as many tables in one TABLES statement as you like. For example, the statements

```
proc freq data=class;
   tables sex race age*sex race*religion;
run;
```

produce two frequency tables and two crosstabulation tables from a data set named CLASS.

To crosstabulate three variables, connect all three variable names with asterisks:

```
proc freq data=class;
   tables age*sex*race;
run;
```

A two-way crosstabulation table of the second and third variables is produced for each value of the first variable.

How PROC FREQ Treats Missing Values

For one-way frequency tables, the number of observations with missing values for a variable appears in the table. For all other tables, missing value frequencies do not appear unless the MISSPRINT option is specified in the TABLES statement. In all cases, statistics do not include missing values unless the MISSING option is specified.

USING PROC MEANS TO SUMMARIZE YOUR DATA

One goal of data analysis is to summarize the data. For example, in your SALES data set, it is difficult to get a complete picture of year-to-date sales by listing all the observations. It would be easier to study the data if you summarized the numbers. You can use PROC MEANS to compute the mean or average year-to-date sales.

PROC MEANS also finds other summary statistics, including the sum, the number of observations, the minimum, and the maximum.

How to Use PROC MEANS

To get summary statistics for all the numeric variables in the SALES data set, use the PROC MEANS statement with a RUN statement (**Screen 6.27**). The results are shown in **Screen 6.28**.

```
┌PROGRAM EDITOR─────────────────────────────────────────────────────┐
│Command ===>                                                        │
│                                                                    │
│00001 proc means data=sales;                                        │
│00002 run;                                                          │
│00003                                                               │
│00004                                                               │
│00005                                                               │
│00006                                                               │
│00007                                                               │
│00008                                                               │
│00009                                                               │
│00010                                                               │
│00011                                                               │
│00012                                                               │
│00013                                                               │
│00014                                                               │
│00015                                                               │
│00016                                                               │
│00017                                                               │
│00018                                                               │
│00019                                                               │
│00020                                                               │
│00021                                                         ZOOM  │
└────────────────────────────────────────────────────────────────────┘
```

Screen 6.27 SAS Statements to Obtain Summary Statistics

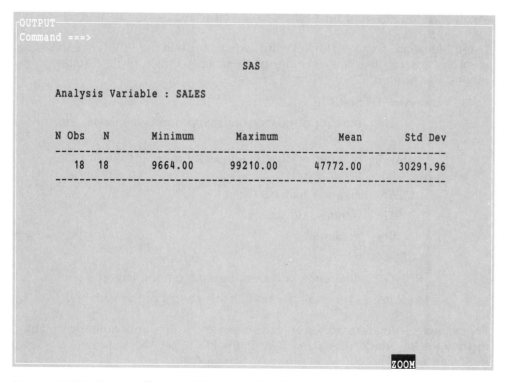

```
┌OUTPUT─────────────────────────────────────────────────────────────┐
│Command ===>                                                        │
│                                                                    │
│                              SAS                                   │
│                                                                    │
│     Analysis Variable : SALES                                      │
│                                                                    │
│                                                                    │
│     N Obs   N      Minimum      Maximum        Mean      Std Dev   │
│     ---------------------------------------------------------------│
│       18   18      9664.00     99210.00     47772.00    30291.96   │
│     ---------------------------------------------------------------│
│                                                                    │
│                                                                    │
│                                                                    │
│                                                                    │
│                                                                    │
│                                                              ZOOM  │
└────────────────────────────────────────────────────────────────────┘
```

Screen 6.28 Report Showing Summary Statistics

To get summary statistics for the most recently created data set, omit DATA=
in the PROC MEANS statement:

```
proc means;
run;
```

In our example, SALES is the only numeric variable in the data set. If your data
set contains many numeric variables and you want to get summary statistics from
some but not all of them, list the variables you want in a VAR statement:

```
proc means;
    var height weight;
run;
```

Statistics You Get Automatically

PROC MEANS automatically prints six statistics for each variable: the total number of observations in the group (marked N Obs in the output), the number of
observations that have valid data for the variable and on which the calculations
are based (N), the minimum (Minimum), the maximum (Maximum), the mean
(Mean), and the standard deviation (Std Dev). **Screen 6.29** shows the default statistics for the SALES variable in the SALES data set.

Selecting Statistics

You can ask the SAS System to print only the summary statistics you need. Corresponding to each PROC MEANS statistic is a keyword. In the PROC MEANS statement, give the keyword for each statistic you want.

Listed below are some of the keywords you can use in the PROC MEANS statement. When you use one or more of these keywords, only the statistics you
request are printed.

Keyword	Statistic
N	number of observations with nonmissing value for the variable
NMISS	number of observations with missing value for the variable
MEAN	mean or average
STD	standard deviation
MIN	minimum
MAX	maximum
RANGE	difference between the smallest and largest values
SUM	sum of all the nonmissing values of the variable.

For example, if you want to see only the mean and sum of your numeric variables,
include the keywords MEAN and SUM in the PROC MEANS statement as shown
in **Screen 6.29**. The output is shown in **Screen 6.30**.

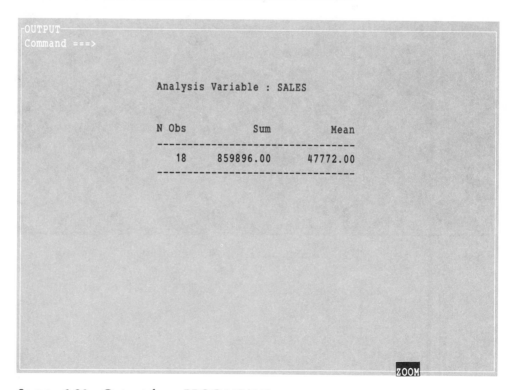

```
┌PROGRAM EDITOR────────────────────────────────────────────
Command ===>

00001 proc means sum mean data=sales;
00002 run;
00003
00004
00005
00006
00007
00008
00009
00010
00011
00012
00013
00014
00015
00016
00017
00018
00019
00020
00021                                                   ZOOM
```

Screen 6.29   SAS Statements to Get Selected Statistics

```
┌OUTPUT────────────────────────────────────────────────────
Command ===>


                  Analysis Variable : SALES


           N Obs          Sum           Mean
           ------------------------------------
             18       859896.00       47772.00
           ------------------------------------








                                                      ZOOM
```

Screen 6.30   Output from PROC MEANS

Getting Subset Means

You can get summary statistics for subsets of your data with PROC MEANS and a BY statement. For example, say you want to get the mean sales first for computers then for small machines. If the data have not been sorted by machine, use the SORT procedure first. Then use a BY MACHINE statement with PROC MEANS (**Screen 6.31** and **Screen 6.32**).

How PROC MEANS Handles Missing Values

Missing values are not included in any calculations that PROC MEANS does. For example, suppose our data set contains a new sales representative named Smith, who has no sales. Smith's observation, therefore, has a missing value for SALES. All statistics for SALES would be calculated from the observations with nonmissing SALES values. If the data set included another numeric variable that had no missing values, all observations would be used to calculate statistics for that variable.

```
┌PROGRAM EDITOR─────────────────────────────────────────────────┐
 Command ===>

 00001 proc sort data=sales;
 00002    by machine;
 00003 run;
 00004 proc means;
 00005    by machine;
 00006 run;
 00007
 00008
 00009
 00010
 00011
 00012
 00013
 00014
 00015
 00016
 00017
 00018
 00019
 00020
 00021
                                                          ZOOM─
```

Screen 6.31   Using PROC MEANS and a BY Statement to Get Summary Statistics

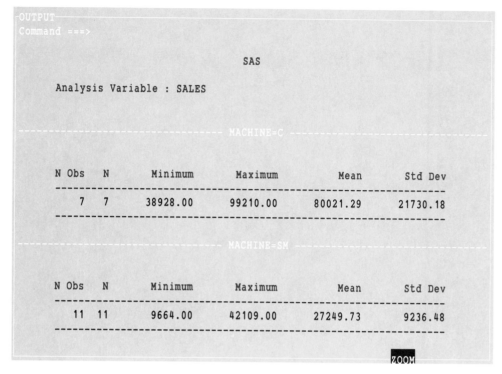

Screen 6.32   Output Showing Summary Statistics

ENVIRONMENT FOR YOUR SAS® SESSION

SAS® Display Manager System

Using the SAS® Procedure Menu System

Chapter 7

SAS® Display Manager System

The earlier chapter "Sample SAS Session" serves as an introduction to the SAS Display Manager System. If you followed the step-by-step example in that chapter, then you should be familiar with display manager as an environment for the SAS System. This chapter contains some additional details about display manager so that you can begin using the SAS System. You can find a complete reference to the SAS Display Manager System in the *SAS Language Guide, Release 6.03 Edition*.

SPECIAL KEYS

In addition to the function keys that you used to execute display manager commands in the "Sample SAS Session," your keyboard includes other editing and cursor keys. Some of the more useful ones are described below. Ask your system administrator to help you locate these keys on your terminal.

 The ENTER or carriage-return key either executes a command or moves the cursor to the first field after the current line.

 The INSERT key inserts characters in text during editing, shifting characters to the right.

The DELETE key erases the character at the current cursor position, shifting any remaining characters to the left.

 The HOME key moves the cursor to the command line in the current active window, which is the window containing the cursor.

 The BACKSPACE key moves the cursor back, erasing characters as it moves.

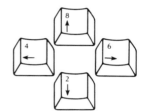 CURSOR keys move the cursor one position to the right, left, up, or down.

SAS DISPLAY MANAGER COMMAND CONVENTIONS

Command Syntax

Descriptions of display manager window commands follow these conventions:

COMMAND OPTION | *option* [OPTION | *option* | ...]

where

CAPITALIZATION
indicates a keyword; you must use the same spelling and form as shown, although you can enter keywords in either uppercase or lowercase.

lowercase italic
indicates you supply the actual value.

vertical bar |
means *or;* use only one of the terms separated by vertical bars.

brackets [ ]
indicate optional information or keywords. Note that you do **not** type in the brackets.

ellipses (...)
mean that more than one of the terms preceding the ellipses can be optionally specified.

The conventions are illustrated in this shortened FIND command description:

FIND *characterstring* [NEXT | ALL]

where

FIND
    is the command keyword.

characterstring
    is a user-supplied value. You type the string of characters you want to locate. Since *characterstring* is not in brackets, you are required to specify it.

[NEXT | ALL]
    are two option keywords that appear in uppercase letters, enclosed by brackets [ ] and separated by vertical bars | . The uppercase letters mean that you enter each exactly as written, although you can enter them in either uppercase or lowercase; the brackets indicate that these options are allowed but not required; the vertical bars indicate that you can specify only one of the two.

DISPLAY MANAGER GLOBAL COMMANDS

Global commands can be executed from the command line or with a function key in any window in the SAS Display Manager System. The global commands you use most often are described below by function. For more information on these special windows and others, see Chapter 10 in the *SAS Language Guide, Release 6.03 Edition.*

Window Call Commands

When one of these commands is issued, the window with that name is displayed on the screen and made active. If the window is already on your screen, the command moves the cursor to the window making it the "active" window.

You have already seen how to use the PGM, LOG, and OUTPUT commands to move among the primary display manager windows. In addition, these commands call the special windows:

AF	displays applications developed with SAS/AF software and CBT courses.
CATALOG	displays the directory of SAS catalogs and allows you to manage SAS catalogs and their entries or to create new catalogs.
DIR	displays information about SAS data sets and SAS catalogs stored in a SAS data library.
FILENAME	displays all currently assigned filerefs and the names of the files to which they refer.
FOOTNOTES	displays a menu for entering up to ten footnote lines to appear on procedure or DATA step output and then for browsing those footnotes.
HELP	displays a help facility with information about the SAS System.
KEYS	provides a facility for displaying, altering, and saving function key settings.

LIBNAME   displays all currently assigned librefs and the path names to which they refer.

MENU   displays the SAS Procedures Menu System, an application that uses a series of fill-in-the-blank panels to guide you through the procedures in the SAS System.

NOTEPAD   displays a window for creating and storing "notepads" of supporting documentation or information.

OPTIONS   displays the current settings of SAS options, which you can change as well as browse.

SETINIT   displays the currently licensed SAS software and expiration dates.

TITLES   displays a menu for entering up to ten title lines to appear on procedure or data set output and then for browsing those titles.

VAR   displays information about variables in a SAS data set.

Window Management Commands

Window management commands help you use windows more efficiently. Here are two of these commands:

END   removes a window from the screen; note that it cannot be used in the LOG and OUTPUT windows. It is the command you use most often to exit from a special window. (The SUBMIT function key is equivalent.)

ZOOM [ON|OFF]

causes the active window to fill the entire screen, concealing the other windows. Execute the command again to return to the previous screen size, or use the ON and OFF options.

Scrolling Commands

When the window contains more information than the physical screen can display at one time, you can scroll the contents of the window with the following scrolling commands:

n

scrolls line n to the top of the window.

BACKWARD [PAGE|HALF|MAX|n]
FORWARD [PAGE|HALF|MAX|n]
LEFT [PAGE|HALF|MAX|n]
RIGHT [PAGE|HALF|MAX|n]

moves the contents of the window backward, forward, left, or right. You can also specify the amount to scroll: PAGE, for the entire amount showing in the window; HALF, for half the amount showing in the window; MAX, the first or last line to the top of the window; n, for n lines or spaces.

TOP
BOTTOM

scrolls to the first line (TOP) or last line (BOTTOM) in the window.

SAS TEXT EDITOR

The SAS text editor provides you with a powerful full-screen editor available in the SAS Display Manager System and in SAS/FSP and SAS/AF software. With the text editor, you can use command-line commands to scroll the contents of a window, to manage your files, to change the color of fields, to assign highlighting attributes, to search for strings, and to move and store text. You can also use line commands to move, copy, delete, and insert data lines. Many of these commands previously belonged to the PROGRAM EDITOR window, and others are new. For a complete list of text editor commands, see Chapter 10, "The SAS Display Manager System," in the *SAS Language Guide*.

Line Commands

These are some of the line commands you will find useful for editing your SAS sessions:

A,B   Mark the target position of one or more lines being moved or copied with a C, M, CC, MM, or INCLUDE command. Indicate an A (after) on the line number of the line you want the source line(s) to follow. Use a B (before) to mark the line you want the source line(s) to precede.

C, CC   To copy one or more lines to another location in the file, place a C on the line number of one line to be copied or indicate CC on the line numbers of the first and last lines of a block of lines to be copied. Then indicate an A on the number of the line you want the copied line(s) to follow or a B on the number of the line you want them to precede.

D, DD   Place a D on the line number of a line you want to delete. To delete a block of lines, place DD on the line numbers of the first and last lines in the block.

I[n]   Use the I line command to insert a new line. To insert *n* lines, type an I followed by the number of lines you want to insert followed by a blank.

M, MM   Use the M or MM command to move a line or block of lines. The move command works just like the C and CC commands except that lines are moved instead of copied.

>[n], >>[n]   Use a > or a > followed by a number (*n*) and a blank space to shift a line of text to the right. To shift a block of text to the right, use >> or >> followed by a number and a blank space on the first and last lines of the block to be shifted. The default is one space.

<[n], <<[n]   Use a < or a < followed by a number (*n*) and a blank space to shift a line of text to the left. To shift a block of text to the left, use << or << followed by a number and a blank space on the first and last lines of the block to be shifted. The default is one space.

R, RR[n]   Use the R or RR command to repeat a line or block of
text. To repeat a line of text more than once, follow R
with a number and a blank space. To repeat a block of
text more than once, follow RR with a number and a
blank space on the first and last lines of the block to be
repeated.

For example, to insert a new line for entering text, type I, the insert line command,
on any part of a line number, like this:

```
0i001 data line one
00002 data line two
00003 data line three
```

and press ENTER. One new line is inserted between the first and second lines.

```
00001 data line one
00002 _
00003 data line two
00004 data line three
```

To move or copy single lines or blocks of lines, you need to indicate the location
where the text is to be moved. The following lines show how to use the M (move)
and A (after) line commands:

```
m0001 Move this line
a0002 after the second line
00003 with the m (move) and a (after) line commands.
```

When you press ENTER, the first line becomes the second line:

```
00001 after the second line
00002 Move this line
00003 with the m (move) and a (after) line commands.
```

You can also use line commands to affect blocks of lines, as in this example:

```
cc001 Copy the first two lines
cc002 after the third line
a0003 with the cc (copy) and a (after) line commands.
```

When you press ENTER, lines one and two are copied after line three:

```
00001 Copy the first two lines
00002 after the third line
00003 with the cc (copy) and a (after) line commands.
00004 Copy the first two lines
00005 after the third line
```

SEARCHING FOR CHARACTER STRINGS

When you are browsing the PROGRAM EDITOR, LOG, or OUTPUT window,
it is useful to be able to search for each occurrence of a character string.

CHANGE and FIND Commands

The CHANGE and FIND commands are similar; use CHANGE in the PROGRAM
EDITOR window to change each occurrence of a string to another string, and
FIND in any of the three windows to find each occurrence of a string. Many of
the options used on the commands for completely specifying the string are the
same.

CHANGE *string1* *string2* [NEXT | FIRST | LAST | PREV | ALL]
 [WORD | PREFIX | SUFFIX]
  Use the CHANGE command when you want to change one or more
  occurrences of *string1* to *string2*. After the keyword CHANGE, give the
  string of characters to be changed, a space, and then the new string.

FIND *characterstring* [NEXT | FIRST | LAST | PREV | ALL]
 [WORD | PREFIX | SUFFIX]
  Use the FIND command to search for a string of characters.

Command Options for Completely Specifying a Character String

In both commands you can tell the system to search for the

- next occurrence of the specified string after the current cursor location
- first occurrence of the string in the file, regardless of your current cursor location
- last occurrence of the string in the file, regardless of your current cursor location
- previous occurrence
- all occurrences.

When the NEXT, FIRST, LAST, or PREV option is specified in the CHANGE command, the specific occurrence is changed. If you specify ALL in the CHANGE command, all occurrences of *string1* are changed to *string2*. When ALL is specified in the FIND command, you receive a message that reports how many times the string occurs in the entire file. When you do not tell the system which occurrence you want, both commands find the next occurrence of the string.

You can also specify one of the following options: PREFIX, SUFFIX, or WORD. If you do not specify one of these options, the system searches for each occurrence of the string, regardless of context.

In the CHANGE or FIND command, a WORD is one or more symbols preceded and followed by a delimiter. A delimiter is any symbol other than an uppercase letter, a lowercase letter, a digit, or an underscore. For example,

ABC123

is a word, but

ABC$123

is two words separated by the delimiter $. The option PREFIX or SUFFIX is treated just as its grammatical definition. In the first example, ABC123, ABC is a prefix and 123 is a suffix. In the second example, ABC$123, ABC and 123 are words, not a prefix and a suffix.

Special Characters and Embedded Blanks

When the string you want to find or change includes special characters or embedded blanks, use single or double quotes to enclose the strings. The first example requires no quotation marks:

```
f yours
c your my
```

The second example does:

```
f 'your data set'
C 'your data set' 'my data set'
```

Also enclose your string in quotes if you have executed the command CAPS ON and you do not want lowercase letters in the string translated into uppercase letters. (The CAPS command is described in the *SAS Language Guide*.) For example, if you have executed the CAPS ON command, the following command finds BOB instead of Bob:

```
f Bob
```

To find Bob with CAPS on, use this command:

```
f 'Bob'
```

If your string contains a single quote, enclose the string in double quotes as in the following examples:

```
f "Bob's"
c "Bob's" "Bill's"
```

RCHANGE and RFIND Commands

The RCHANGE and RFIND commands allow you to continue searching for or changing strings without having to reenter CHANGE or FIND commands. RCHANGE and RFIND commands are normally associated with function keys.

RCHANGE   Use the RCHANGE command to continue to find and change a string of characters previously specified in a CHANGE command.

RFIND   Use the RFIND command to continue to search for a string of characters previously specified in a FIND or CHANGE command.

You can combine the use of the CHANGE command and RFIND command. For example, after you enter a CHANGE command, you can press the RFIND function key to locate the next occurrence of *string1* before pressing RCHANGE to change it to *string2*.

Using CHANGE and FIND Commands in Display Manager Windows

Suppose that after you enter your SAS statements and data shown in **Screen 7.1**, you want to change all occurrences of 'SM' to 'S' in the data lines. Use the CHANGE command on the command line.

```
┌PROGRAM EDITOR─────────────────────────────────────────────────────┐
│Command ===> change SM S all                                        │
│                                                                    │
│00001 data sales;                                                   │
│00002    input salesrep $ sales region $ machine $;                 │
│00003    cards;                                                     │
│00004 Stafer     9664    east      SM                               │
│00005 Young      22969   east      SM                               │
│00006 Stride     27253   east      SM                               │
│00007 Topin      86432   east      C                                │
│00008 Spark      99210   east      C                                │
│00009 Vetter     38928   west      C                                │
│00010 Curci      21531   west      SM                               │
│00011 Marco      79345   west      C                                │
│00012 Greco      18523   west      SM                               │
│00013 Ryan       32915   west      SM                               │
│00014 Tomas      42109   west      SM                               │
│00015 Thalman    94320   south     C                                │
│00016 Moore      25718   south     SM                               │
│00017 Allen      64700   south     C                                │
│00018 Stelam     27634   south     SM                               │
│00019 Farlow     32719   north     SM                               │
│00020 Smith      38712   north     SM                               │
│00021 Wilson     97214   north     C                                │
│                                                          ─ZOOM─    │
└────────────────────────────────────────────────────────────────────┘
```

Screen 7.1 Using the CHANGE Command

When you press ENTER, the data values are changed (**Screen 7.2**).

```
┌PROGRAM EDITOR─────────────────────────────────────────────────────┐
│Command ===>                                                        │
│NOTE: Changed 11 occurrence(s) of the string.                       │
│00001 data sales;                                                   │
│00002    input salesrep $ sales region $ machine $;                 │
│00003    cards;                                                     │
│00004 Stafer     9664    east      S                                │
│00005 Young      22969   east      S                                │
│00006 Stride     27253   east      S                                │
│00007 Topin      86432   east      C                                │
│00008 Spark      99210   east      C                                │
│00009 Vetter     38928   west      C                                │
│00010 Curci      21531   west      S                                │
│00011 Marco      79345   west      C                                │
│00012 Greco      18523   west      S                                │
│00013 Ryan       32915   west      S                                │
│00014 Tomas      42109   west      S                                │
│00015 Thalman    94320   south     C                                │
│00016 Moore      25718   south     S                                │
│00017 Allen      64700   south     C                                │
│00018 Stelam     27634   south     S                                │
│00019 Farlow     32719   north     S                                │
│00020 Smith      38712   north     S                                │
│00021 Wilson     97214   north     C                                │
│                                                          ─ZOOM─    │
└────────────────────────────────────────────────────────────────────┘
```

Screen 7.2 Changed Data Values

Suppose you want to scroll through the system messages in a SAS LOG window like that shown in **Screen 7.3**. Enter the FIND command on the command line and press ENTER. The cursor moves to the first occurrence of the word NOTE. To find the next occurrence, use the RFIND command or key.

```
OUTPUT
Command ===>




















LOG
Command ===> find NOTE


     3    cards;
    22    run;
NOTE: The data set WORK.SALES has 18 observations and 4 variables.
NOTE: The DATA statement used 16.00 seconds.
PROGRAM EDITOR
Command ===>

00001
00002
00003
```

Screen 7.3   Using the FIND Command

HELP WINDOW

A series of HELP windows makes the SAS System especially convenient. When you execute the HELP command from one of the three primary windows, you get information about the SAS System, for example information about SAS procedures and display manager windows. If you execute HELP from one of the special windows, such as the NOTEPAD window, information about using that window is displayed. The HELP window has two types of panels: menu panels and help panels.

Suppose that you are entering SAS statements in the PROGRAM EDITOR window and need help with a SAS procedure. Enter the HELP command on the command line of the PROGRAM EDITOR and press ENTER or press the HELP function key.

On the command line of the HELP menu enter the number or name of the item for which you want help and press ENTER. You can go several levels deep, depending on the amount of information you need about the subject. To return to the primary menu panel from any other panel, enter an equal sign (=) on the command line and press ENTER. To return to the previous panel, use the END command. If you are on the primary menu panel, the END command removes the HELP window from the screen.

Chapter 8

Using the SAS®
Procedure Menu
System

The SAS Procedure Menu System, part of the SAS System for Personal Computers, is designed to make SAS procedures easy to use for everyone from novice SAS users to experienced programmers. The system is composed of menus or fill-in-the-blank panels that guide you through the procedures in the SAS System. The panels follow actual SAS procedure syntax, providing prompts in the form of SAS statements. By following the syntax on the panels, new users can learn how to use SAS procedures, casual users no longer need to memorize the options they like to use, and programmers have at their fingertips the skeleton of any SAS procedure they need to use.

Selecting a SAS Procedure

To use the SAS Procedure Menu System to prepare your SAS procedure statements, invoke the SAS System with display manager in effect. On the command line of any window, enter

    menu autosave=yes

and press the ENTER key. (You can also hold down the CTRL key and press A.) You can issue the MENU command from any window in display manager. If you receive an error message, check with your SAS Software Representative to be sure that the SAS Procedure Menu System has been installed correctly. **Screen 8.1** shows the Primary Procedure Menu, the first screen displayed.

```
┌SAS PROCEDURE MENU SYSTEM──────────────────────────────────────────
│ Select Option ===>
│
│               S A S   P R O C E D U R E   M E N U   S Y S T E M
│
│
│        BASE              UTILITIES            REMOTE LINK
│
│        CALENDAR          APPEND               DOWNLOAD
│        CHART             CATALOG   (use 1)    UPLOAD
│        CORR              CIMPORT              SIGNON        (use 3)
│        FORMS             COMPARE              SIGNOFF       (use 4)
│        FREQ              CONTENTS
│        MEANS             COPY
│        PLOT              CPORT                OTHER SAS PRODUCTS
│        PRINT             DATASETS
│        RANK              DBF                  SAS/STAT      (use STAT)
│        STANDARD          DIF                  SAS/GRAPH     (use GRAPH)
│        SUMMARY           FORMAT               SAS/FSP       (use FSP)
│        TABULATE          OPTIONS   (use 2)    SAS/AF        (use 5)
│        TIMEPLOT          PRINTTO
│        TRANSPOSE         SORT
│        UNIVARIATE                             TYPE H FOR HELP
│
│
```

Screen 8.1   Primary Procedure Menu

Notice that the procedures are grouped by category for easier use. You can find complete descriptions of these procedures in the appropriate SAS System documentation.* For information on how to use the procedures in the Remote Link category, refer to the *SAS Guide to the Micro-to-Host Link, Version 6 Edition*. You can return to display manager at any time from the Primary Procedure Menu by typing END on the command line or by pressing the END function key.

To select a procedure, enter the name of the procedure on the command line and press the ENTER key. For example, to select the MEANS procedure, type MEANS on the command line and press the ENTER key to display the MEANS procedure panel (**Screen 8.2**). If a procedure panel takes up more than one screen, a message appears on the screen. Use the FORWARD and BACKWARD keys to see the entire panel.

---

* The menu will change as additional procedures and products are added to the SAS System, and some procedures listed may be part of a SAS software product you do not have.

```
┌─MEANS: Computes descriptive statistics─────────────────────────────────┐
│ Command ===>                                                           │
│                                                                        │
│   PROC MEANS    DATA =                          Input data set         │
│                        ------------------                              │
│   Choose statistics for printed analysis:                              │
│   N  [_]     NMISS  [_]     MEAN [_]    STD [_]    MIN [_]    MAX [_]    │
│   T  [_]     SUMWGT [_]     VAR  [_]    USS [_]    CSS [_]              │
│   CV [_]     STDERR [_]     RANGE [_]   PRT [_]    SUM [_]        ;      │
│                                                                        │
│   VAR     ..............................................................; │
│           Numeric variables to be analyzed                             │
│                                                                        │
│   CLASS   ..............................................................; │
│           Grouping variables                                           │
│                                                                        │
│   ID      ..............................................................; │
│           Variables whose values are to identify observations          │
│                                                                        │
│   BY      ..............................................................; │
│           BY variables                                                 │
│                                                                        │
│ Enter SUBMIT to run, CANCEL to quit without running, PAGE DOWN for more │
└────────────────────────────────────────────────────────────────────────┘
```

Screen 8.2   Panel for MEANS Procedure

Browsing a Procedure Panel

Each procedure panel lists keywords for SAS statements and options, as well as comments and instructional text. On a PC with a color display, the keywords, fields, and instructional text appear in different colors for easier reading. In the designated fields, you enter information (for example, the name of a data set or variable names) or select options (by placing an X in the blank beside the option). If you want to use the default value for an option, leave the field beside the option blank. After you enter the necessary information and select the options you want to use, you are ready to submit the statements to the SAS System for execution. You can return to the Primary Procedure Menu from a procedure panel without executing the statements you have requested by entering the CANCEL command and pressing the ENTER key.

To check the completed statements before you submit them, press the ENTER key. The SAS Procedure Menu System checks most of the information and action fields to be sure that the information is correct. If any of the information is incorrect (for example, if you misspell the name of a data set or enter the name of a variable that is not in the data set), you receive a message. You should reenter the information and press the ENTER key again.

To submit the statements to the SAS System, type SUBMIT on the command line and press the ENTER key, or press the SUBMIT function key. If you forget to fill in any required information, you receive a message when you try to execute your statements, and the cursor is positioned for you on the required field. Simply supply the necessary information and resubmit your statements.

If you are unfamiliar with the syntax for a procedure, enter

```
help
```

on the command line of the procedure for a quick on-line help reference, or refer to the SAS System documentation for that procedure.

You can use various commands on the procedure panels to assist you in completing the panels. These commands are described with the MENU window in Chapter 7, "The SAS Display Manager System."

Filling in a Procedure Panel

To see how easy it is to use the SAS Procedure Menu System, you can begin by filling in the PROC MEANS panel and submitting the statements to the SAS System. First, supply the name of a data set in the DATA= field. This example uses a data set named SALES, but you can supply the name of any SAS data set. If you are using a permanent SAS data set, be sure that you have made the data set available to your session and use a two-level name in the DATA= field. If you leave the DATA= field blank, the last SAS data set created is used.

If you want to get summary statistics for all the numeric variables in the SALES data set (the default), you can fill in the DATA= field and submit this panel to the SAS System without filling in any other fields. Press the SUBMIT function key or enter the SUBMIT command on the command line and press ENTER. The MENU window is closed and the OUTPUT, LOG, and PROGRAM EDITOR windows are displayed. The procedure output appears in the OUTPUT window (**Screen 8.3**).

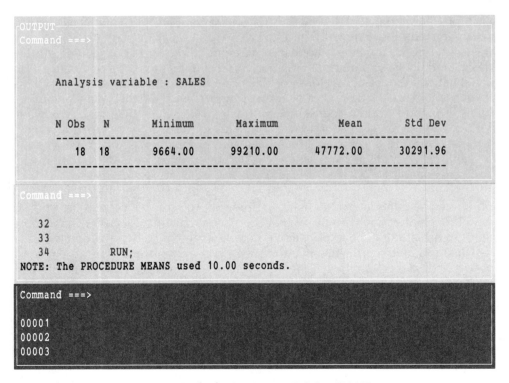

Screen 8.3   Output Using Default Options: PROC MEANS

After viewing your output, enter the MENU command on any of the command lines and press ENTER. The Primary Procedure Menu reappears. To execute another procedure, type its name on the command line of the menu as you did before.

Suppose you want to run the MEANS procedure again, but with options you select. To run the procedure again, type the name MEANS on the command line of the menu and press ENTER. The MEANS procedure panel is displayed. You can then use the RECALL command to recall the statements you completed in the previous panel for that procedure.* Enter RECALL on the command line and press ENTER, or press the RECALL function key.

This time, suppose you want to see only the mean and the sum of the numeric variables in the SALES data set. The name of the data set has already been filled in for you. Place Xs in the blanks beside the MEAN and SUM options. You can submit this panel to the SAS System by pressing the SUBMIT function key or by entering the SUBMIT command and pressing ENTER. The output is shown in **Screen 8.4**.

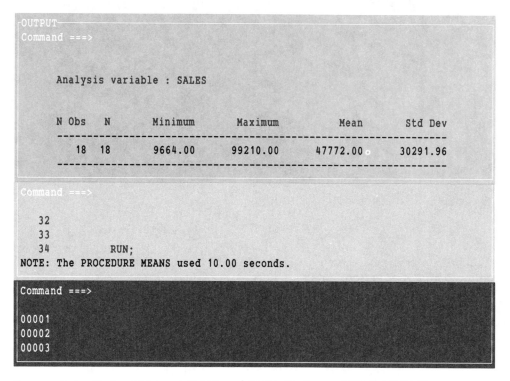

Screen 8.4   Output Using MEAN and SUM Options: PROC MEANS

After viewing your output, reenter the menu system by typing MENU on the command line and pressing ENTER.

---

*   The statements are available because you used the AUTOSAVE=YES option, either by typing it with the MENU command or as part of the CTRL-A function key, when you originally invoked the Procedure Menu System.

Suppose you want to run PROC MEANS again, but this time you want to get the mean sales first for computers (where the variable MACHINE has the value C) and then for small machines (the value SM). First, you need to sort the SALES data set by MACHINE before you use PROC MEANS. On the Primary Procedure Menu, select the SORT procedure by typing SORT on the command line and pressing ENTER. The PROC SORT panel appears, as shown in **Screen 8.5**.

```
 ┌SORT: Sorts a data set─────────────────────────────────────────────
 │Command ===>


            PROC SORT    DATA =                        Input data set
                                 ------------------
                         OUT  =                        Output data set
                                 ------------------

            Options:
               NODUPKEY [_]    Eliminates observations with identical keys
               TAGSORT  [_]    Saves disk space but it is slower


            BY  .........................................  ;  REQUIRED FIELD
                    Variables that supply sort keys




            Enter SUBMIT to run, CANCEL to quit without running
```

Screen 8.5   Panel for SORT Procedure

You can enter the name of your data set, SALES, in the DATA= field. Next, fill in the name of an output data set in the OUT= field so that you can keep your original data set and the new one you are creating. In this example, the new data set is called SALESORT, so enter the name SALESORT in the OUT= field. Remember, if you are using a permanent SAS data set as input, you must use a two-level name in the DATA= field. Also, if you want to store your sorted data set for later use, use a two-level name in the OUT= field. Since you want to sort your data by the variable MACHINE, enter the variable name MACHINE in the BY field. When you are finished, your screen looks like the one shown in **Screen 8.6**.

```
┌─SORT: Sorts a data set──────────────────────────────────────────────────
│ Command ===>
│
│
│
│          PROC SORT    DATA =  sales                      Input data set
│                               ------------------
│                       OUT  =  salesort                   Output data set
│                               ------------------
│
│          Options:
│             NODUPKEY [_]     Eliminates observations with identical keys
│             TAGSORT  [_]     Saves disk space but it is slower
│
│
│          BY  machine.................................  ;  REQUIRED FIELD
│              Variables that supply sort keys
│
│
│
│
│
│
│          Enter SUBMIT to run, CANCEL to quit without running
│
│
```

Screen 8.6   Completed Panel for SORT Procedure

What if you don't remember the name of the variable that contains the type of machine? In that case, enter a question mark in the BY field (**Screen 8.7**).

```
┌SORT: Sorts a data set──────────────────────────────────────────
│Command ===>


        PROC SORT   DATA =  sales                   Input data set
                            ------------------
                    OUT  =  salesort                Output data set
                            ------------------


        Options:
            NODUPKEY [_]   Eliminates observations with identical keys
            TAGSORT  [_]   Saves disk space but it is slower


        BY  ?........................................  ;  REQUIRED FIELD
             Variables that supply sort keys




        Enter SUBMIT to run, CANCEL to quit without running
```

Screen 8.7   Asking for a List of Variables

A list of variables in the data set appears (**Screen 8.8**). The variable you want is MACHINE, so move the cursor to that name and press ENTER. The name becomes highlighted. If you change your mind, move the cursor back to that name and press ENTER again; the selection is released and the highlighting disappears. Press the END function key or type END on the command line to end the selection panel. You return to the SORT procedure panel, and the name you selected has been copied into the BY field.

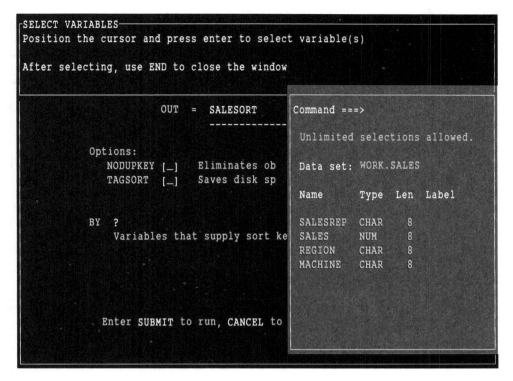

```
┌SELECT VARIABLES─────────────────────────────────────────────────
 Position the cursor and press enter to select variable(s)

 After selecting, use END to close the window


                    OUT  =  SALESORT      Command ===>
                            ------------
                                          Unlimited selections allowed.
            Options:
              NODUPKEY [_]    Eliminates ob  Data set: WORK.SALES
              TAGSORT  [_]    Saves disk sp
                                            Name      Type  Len  Label

            BY  ?                           SALESREP  CHAR   8
                  Variables that supply sort ke  SALES     NUM    8
                                            REGION    CHAR   8
                                            MACHINE   CHAR   8




            Enter SUBMIT to run, CANCEL to
```

Screen 8.8   Selecting a Variable

Now you can press the SUBMIT function key or enter the SUBMIT command and press ENTER. The SORT procedure produces no printed output, but the LOG window contains a message that your data set has been sorted.

You may want to verify that the data set was sorted properly, so enter

    menu print

on the command line and press ENTER. The menu system bypasses the Primary Procedure Menu and displays the PRINT procedure panel, as shown in **Screen 8.9**.

```
┌─PRINT: Prints a SAS data set.─────────────────────────────────────┐
│Command ===>                                                       │
│                                                                   │
│  PROC PRINT     DATA =                        Input data set      │
│                         ------------------                        │
│  Options:    LABEL   [_]   Use variables' labels as column headings│
│              SPLIT = '_'   Split character (implies the LABEL option)│
│              N       [_]   Print number of observations           │
│                                                                   │
│     ID          ..................................................;│
│              Variables whose values are to identify observations  │
│              NOOBS  [_]   Suppress printing of observation number │
│                                                                   │
│     BY          machine..........................................;│
│              By variables                                         │
│                                                                   │
│     SUM         ..................................................;│
│              Variables whose values are to be totaled             │
│              ROUND  [_]   Round variables in SUM or SUMBY statements│
│                                                                   │
│     VAR         ..................................................;│
│              Print only these variables                           │
│  Enter SUBMIT to run, CANCEL to quit without running, PAGE DOWN for more│
│                                                                   │
└───────────────────────────────────────────────────────────────────┘
```

Screen 8.9   Panel for PRINT Procedure

To see what your new data set, SALESORT, looks like, you can fill in the PRINT procedure panel. The procedure automatically uses the most recently created data set (in this example, SALESORT), so you can leave the DATA= field blank. Next, since you sorted your data set by the variable MACHINE, you want to print it using MACHINE as your BY variable. Fill in MACHINE in the BY field. When you have filled in the fields you need, the procedure panel looks like the one shown in **Screen 8.10**.

When you press the SUBMIT function key or enter the SUBMIT command and press ENTER, your statements are executed, and the output for the PRINT procedure appears in the OUTPUT window. Use the ZOOM command to make the output fill the entire screen if you want, and use the FORWARD and BACKWARD commands to move through the output (**Screen 8.11**).

```
┌PRINT: Prints a sas data set.─────────────────────────────────────────┐
│Command ===>                                                          │
│                                                                      │
│  PROC PRINT     DATA =                         Input data set        │
│                          ------------------                          │
│  Options:     LABEL    [_]    Use variables' labels as column headings│
│               SPLIT = '_'    Split character (implies the LABEL option)│
│               N        [_]    Print number of observations            │
│                                                                      │
│      ID         .........................................................; │
│               Variables whose values are to identify observations     │
│               NOOBS   [_]    Suppress printing of observation number  │
│                                                                      │
│      BY         machine.................................................; │
│               By variables                                            │
│                                                                      │
│      SUM        .........................................................; │
│               Variables whose values are to be totaled                │
│               ROUND   [_]    Round variables in SUM or SUMBY statements│
│                                                                      │
│      VAR        .........................................................; │
│               Print only these variables                              │
│                                           PAGE DOWN FOR MORE          │
└──────────────────────────────────────────────────────────────────────┘
```

Screen 8.10   Completed Panel for PRINT Procedure

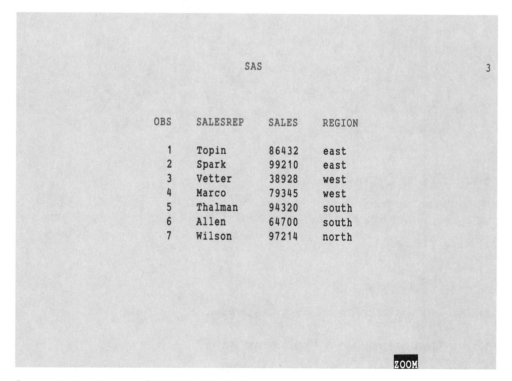

Screen 8.11   Zoomed PROC PRINT Output

Now you are ready to run the MEANS procedure again using the sorted data set. Return to the Primary Procedure Menu and select the MEANS procedure. When the procedure panel appears, fill in the appropriate information. Enter the name SALESORT in the DATA= field, place an X in the blank beside the MEAN option to get mean sales, and enter the variable MACHINE in the BY statement field. Press the ENTER key to have the SAS Procedure Menu System check all the information for accuracy; then submit your statements to the SAS System. The zoomed output from PROC MEANS is shown in **Screen 8.12**.

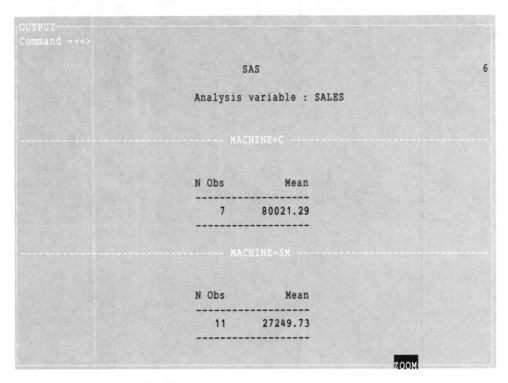

Screen 8.12   Zoomed Output from PROC MEANS

Saving Your Output

If you want to save your procedure output, you can use the FILE command to write the output to a file. On the command line of the output window, enter

    file fileref

or

    file 'actualfilename'

and the output is sent to the file you specified.

Using Commands on a Procedure Panel

To issue a command in a procedure panel, either type the command on the command line and press ENTER, or use a function key (either a key defined by the SAS System or one that you define). You can use all the commands listed in **Display Manager Global Commands** and in the **MENU Window** in Chapter 10, "The SAS Display Manager System," in the *SAS Language Guide for Personal Computers, Release 6.03 Edition*.

Index

Your Turn

If you have comments about SAS software or the *SAS Introductory Guide for Personal Computers, Release 6.03 Edition*, please send them to us on a photocopy of this page.

Please return the photocopy to the Publications Division (for comments about this book) or the Technical Support Division (for suggestions about the software) at SAS Institute, SAS Campus Drive, Cary, NC 27513.